MW00426298

PREDATOR ON THE DIAMOND: THE BOSTON RED SOX YOUTH MOLESTATION STORY

Copyright © 2012 by Gary G. Tavares
Printed by Kindle Direct Publishing
Cover graphics by Richard Anthony Evans
Published by Tavares Entertainment, LLC.:

Gary G. Tavares
Tavares Entertainment, LLC.
3320 S. Cobb Drive SE #21
Smyrna, GA 30080
678-437-4496
docperformer@hotmail.com
www.tavaresentertainment.net

ISBN: 978-0-9833292-5-1

Gary G. Tavares

PREFACE

"Predator on the Diamond: The Boston Red Sox Youth Molestation Story" could be the most eye-opening and compelling untold story of child molestation, within a sports organization, in sports history. You will see how the circumstances of these young African American boys, who were mostly poor and fatherless, were used to take advantage of them. Take a look into the mind of the predator and see how he uses his position of power to control and manipulate these young victims.

Look into the minds of the actual young victims and see some of the signs of abuse which parents can often overlook. We send them to various professional sports organizations to work with some of the biggest athletes of our time and we assume they are safe. However, how many Penn State scandals are waiting to emerge? How do we protect our youth? The answers to these questions may be more complex than we know but this story may help to bring awareness to this issue.

CHAPTER ONE

The year is 2001 and the place is Winter Haven, Florida. A Psychiatrist, Doctor Ross, a medium sized Caucasian male, sits in his comfortable leather office chair. His office is medium-sized, decorated with certificates and family pictures. He checks his watch and looks up at the clock on his wall. He takes a remote control and clicks his radio on. A Smooth Jazz station comes on and the Doctor starts doing some paperwork. He takes off his suit jacket and loosens his tie a little. The phone rings and he answers it. "Yes, please send the gentleman back," he replies.

The Secretary, an African American female in her twenties, swings Doctor Ross' door open. A medium-built African American man who is thirty-one walks in the office. The man's name is William Jones. Doctor Ross stands up and reaches out to shake William's hand. "How are you doing Mr. Jones?" Doctor Ross asks as he shakes William's hand. "I am okay, I guess; just a little nervous," William said as he shook Doctor Ross' hand firmly.

"Is there anything I can get you Mr. Jones?" the secretary asked. "No thank you, I think I will be fine," William quickly replied. The secretary left, closing the door behind her. The Doctor told William to have a seat and make himself comfortable. William sat in the other very comfortable leather chair and attempted to get comfortable. However, William was clearly nervous as he shifted back and forth and shook his left leg back and forth. William was wearing a suit and began to unbutton his jacket and loosen his tie. "I am sorry, Mr. Jones, but our air conditioning system is definitely not the best. At least it is working though," Doctor Ross said as he arranged some things on his desk.

William leaned back in the chair and told Doctor Ross how comfortable it was. Doctor Ross jokingly told William not to go to sleep on him. Doctor Ross put a small recorder on his desk and took out a letter-sized note pad, along with an ink pen. William just sat there looking around at all the pictures and certificates on the wall. "First things first, Mr. Jones; Now, do you mind if I tape this session?" Doctor Ross asked William. William told the doctor he did not mind if he taped the session. Doctor Ross pushed the button down and said, "I am Doctor Howard Ross, and it is May nineteenth two thousand one. The time is fourteen-hundred hours. I am interviewing William Jones."

PREDATOR ON THE DIAMOND: THE BOSTON RED SOX YOUTH MOLESTATION STORY

"William is one of the many African American men who claim to have been molested while working in the Boston Red Sox organization," he continued. Doctor Ross points at Will and signals him to start the interview. "Well, it all started back in the mid-eighties. I was fifteen years old, but I remember everything like it was yesterday," William said as he stared straight ahead, focused. He began to go back to where it all began.

He went back to the year 1985, at the Chain of Lakes ballpark in Winter Haven, Florida. The Boston Red Sox players warm up and practice at their spring training facility in Winter Haven, Florida. It's a bright and sunny day and the weather is rather warm. The clubhouse Manager, known as Fitzy, leans against the dugout and watches the players practice. Fitzy comes from his last name, which is Fitzpatrick. He is a Caucasian male in his fifties.

He works on the visitor's side. One of the players, who is a Caucasian male in his early twenties, approaches Fitzy. His name is Paul. Paul asks Fitzy to bring him some of the new batting gloves. Some of the new equipment was kept in the clubhouse equipment room. Fitzy turns around and starts to look for one of the clubbies. The young boys who worked in the clubhouse were known as clubbies.

A young black boy, Dave, was carrying some baseball equipment onto the field. "Hey Dave, I need you to do me a favor buddy," Fitzy said as he put his hand on Dave's shoulder. "I need you to run down to the clubhouse locker room and get some of the new batting gloves," Fitzy continued. Dave put down the equipment and jogged towards the clubhouse locker room. "He'll never find those gloves. I will go over to the clubhouse and help him get your gloves," Fitzy said with sort of a grin.

"Thanks Fitzy, I appreciate that," Paul said as he slung his bat over his shoulder and walked away. Inside the equipment room, Dave is looking for the batting gloves. As he goes through the equipment, Fitzy quietly walks into the equipment room. He stands there watching Dave for a while. "You having a little trouble finding those gloves little buddy?" Fitzy asked with sort of a grin on his face. Dave is startled and jumps.

He stares at Fitzy as if he is the grim reaper. He walked towards Dave, and Dave backed up towards one of the equipment storage lockers. Fitzy reaches into one of the top lockers above Dave, opens it and brings out the gloves. Dave just stands there looking at Fitzy. Fitzy puts his free hand on Dave's shoulder and smiles.

"That's okay, buddy. You are doing really well. In fact, I can see you being my top clubby one day. You can even be the clubhouse Manager someday if you keep up the good work," Fitzy said as he encouraged Dave and tried to calm him down. "Thank you, Fitzy," Dave replied as Fitzy patted him on the top of his head and walked away, still smiling. There was a reason Dave did not feel too comfortable when he was alone around Fitzy.

He just could feel there was something about Fitzy that was not right. The way he smiled at him. The way he had to touch Dave every time he spoke to him. Dave wanted to avoid Fitzy, but it was quite difficult, because after all, Fitzy was his boss. Besides, Fitzy treated him and the other clubbies like they were his own kids. He took care of them when many of them had no father figure or strong male role models.

CHAPTER TWO

A vehicle slowly cruised down the streets of an inner-city neighborhood. The neighborhood is near Winter Haven, Florida. Fitzy steps out of the car. There are several young black boys running around and playing in the streets. They all stop what they're doing and practically swarm Fitzy to greet him. Fitzy opens his trunk and pulls out packs of bubble gum, some juices, a few baseballs and other items and hands them to the boys. "Okay who is the strongest out here?" Fitzy asked as he put his own arm up to flex it.

"Let me see some muscles!" Fitzy yelled, almost like a drill sergeant. The boys all practically jump in front of each other and fight for position to show their muscles. "Wow you all are strong. You guys have been eating your Wheaties," Fitzy said as he squeezed a few muscles. Ricky, a twelve-year-old young black boy, comes running up to Fitzy and gives him a hug. "Hello Mr. Fitzpatrick," Ricky says with a big smile as he takes some of the goodies from Fitzy.

PREDATOR ON THE DIAMOND: THE BOSTON RED SOX YOUTH MOLESTATION STORY

"How are you doing little buddy?" Fitzy asked. "I'm fine Mr. Fitzpatrick," Ricky replied as he started tearing the paper away from his candy. Fitzy puts his hand on Ricky's shoulder and starts to walk with him. Fitzy waves to the other boys and says, "Okay gentlemen, I will be right back. I just need to talk to Ricky right now." The boys all scatter and continue playing and doing what they were doing. Fitzy continues to walk and talk with Ricky. Fitzy asked Ricky how his mother was doing. Ricky, after a short pause, said "she is doing fine." Fitzy asked Ricky if he still wanted to come over and work for him at the ballpark.

Ricky said Yes to Mr. Fitzpatrick and seemed to get excited. "Well, how are your grades now buddy?" Fitzy asked as he once again put his hand on Ricky's shoulder. Ricky proudly proclaimed he was getting all A's and B's. Fitzy smiled, hugged Ricky and said, "That's great! I don't see it being a problem for you to work with me then. Your mother just wanted you to pick up your grades. So, have you been eating your Wheaties? I told you to get ready for this job because it is pretty physical." "I am ready Mr. Fitzpatrick," Ricky said with certainty and determination. Fitzy then asked to see his muscles. Ricky quickly slid up the sleeve to his short-sleeved shirt and flexed his muscle.

"See I'm strong Mr. Fitzpatrick!" Ricky said as he waited for Fitzy's approval. "Yeah you are strong. You have been eating your spinach too huh?" Fitzy said as he squeezed Ricky's muscles. Ricky once again told Fitzy he was ready. He was just hoping his mother would let him do this. He sometimes was more than a handful for his mother. Even though he was pretty smart and did well in school, he was a fatherless boy with some emotional problems, which were caused by it. He hoped Fitzy would be able to convince his mother to let him work at the ballpark. "I'm sure you can use a little extra cash to help your mother out," Fitzy said.

Fitzy continued by asking, "By the way, is your mother home?" Ricky told him she was. "Well let's go see what she says buddy," Fitzy said with confidence. Later, at Ricky's house, Ricky's mother, Michelle, flops on the couch and turns on the television. Michelle is a short African American lady in her thirties. Suddenly, there is a knock on the metal screen door. Michelle loudly yells out, "Who is it?" Ricky replied, "Mom it's me and Mr. Fitzpatrick." Michelle pats down her hair and straightens her clothes a bit. She opens the door and says, "I'm sorry Mr. Fitzpatrick I didn't know you were coming by." Fitzy apologized and said, "Michelle is this a bad time? I mean I can come back another time."

PREDATOR ON THE DIAMOND: THE BOSTON RED SOX YOUTH MOLESTATION STORY

Michelle told Fitzy it was okay for him to come in. After all, it was not his first time through the neighborhood, and it was not his first time stopping over Michelle's house. Fitzy was pretty persistent and often made return visits to some of the homes. Sometimes he would recruit several young boys from one household. Michelle moves the newspaper out of the way and turns off the television. She starts picking up some clothes and other items that were lying around. She then flops back down on the couch.

"You can have a seat Mr. Fitzpatrick. Can I get you something?" Michelle asked. Ricky did not need to be told to sit down. He came right in and sat on the couch. He wanted to sit right next to his mother, feeling he could help Fitzy convince her. "Michelle, Michelle, Michelle," Fitzy said as he shook his head. Michelle said, "Yes, Mr. Fitzpatrick." Fitzy reminded her to call him Fitzy. That was really the name most people who knew him, including the clubbies, called him. "I'm sorry Mr. Fitz. . . I mean Fitzy. Well, it's just that I am so used to calling you Mr. Fitzpatrick. I know we have known each other for a while now but..." Michelle said with an apologetic tone.

Fitzy once again reminded her it was what everyone called him, and he was okay with it. She proceeded to ask Fitzy if she could get him anything. "I guess a glass of cold water will be fine thank you," Fitzy said. Michelle goes into the kitchen and pours Fitzy a glass of cold water. She brings the glass of water out and sits it on the coffee table. Fitzy thanked Michelle for the water and immediately began drinking it. "So how can I help you? Oh, let me guess, you want to take Ricky off my hands huh?" Michelle asked. She pretty much knew that was what he was there for. Ricky's other brother was already working at the ballpark and seemed to be doing well.

Fitzy got straight to the point and said, "Last time we spoke you said Ricky could work for me if he brought his grades up and according to him he has done that. I mean I still have a spot for him, and he seems to be a fine young boy." Michelle proudly bragged about how Ricky had brought his grades up and reminded Fitzy jokingly that he is a fine boy most of the time. Fitzy always knew what to say and how to say it to the parents. He always used similar dialogue to convince the child and parent of how great the opportunity would be. He told Michelle how he would earn money and get to work around some great baseball players in a great major league organization.

PREDATOR ON THE DIAMOND: THE BOSTON RED SOX YOUTH MOLESTATION STORY

"Please mom can I go?" Ricky asked with an innocent expression and puppy eyes. "Of course, he can work for you! We all appreciate what you're doing around here. You're taking these boys off the streets and giving them something constructive to do." Ricky jumps around with joy and celebrates like someone who has won the lotto. His mother just looks at him with a serious face and he sits back down on the couch, quickly and quietly. "Well, I do what I can. Most of these young men just need a chance. So, let's get this young man signed up. Believe me you made the right decision," Fitzy said confidently.

Michelle told Fitzy she knew she was making the right decision. She reminded Fitzy, Ricky could work with him as long as he kept his grades up. She said that seriously as she looked back and forth at Fitzy and Ricky. She wanted them both to be clear on that. She did not want this opportunity to be detrimental to his education and him continuing to get good grades. "I'm sure he will do fine. One of these young men might even take my job as clubhouse manager one day. I mean like I said they all have a lot of potential," Fitzy said as he took a gulp of the refreshing cold water. Michelle agreed with him and said, "They just want the easy way out, so they never really learn about their potential."

She continued to say, "By the way, I plan to send his brother Barry your way soon." Fitzy smiled and told Michelle how great it would be for Ricky and his brothers to work together. Fitzy got up and stood at the door watching the kids playing outside. He turned, looked at Michelle and said, "Believe me Michelle, if I could take them all off the streets I would." Michelle, with a very serious expression, replied, "Wouldn't that be great? You see a lot of these boys just need a father or male role model in their lives. Some of them see you as a father figure around here. Hell, some of them see you more than they see their fathers."

Fitzy thanked her and reminded her how long he had been coming through that neighborhood. He said he certainly planned on keeping at it and told Michelle he knew some of these kids before they could walk. Michelle said how the whole neighborhood really appreciates him and she told him he was like family here. Fitzy thanked her once again, looked at his watch and said, "I guess I better get going." Fitzy rubs Ricky on the top of his head and says, "You're going to be a good clubby. Just keep those grades up."

PREDATOR ON THE DIAMOND: THE BOSTON RED SOX YOUTH MOLESTATION STORY

CHAPTER THREE

It is a bright and sunny morning in Winter Haven, Florida. At the Jones family house, there are four children that still live at home. They are Jimmy 20, Larry 18, William 15 and Lisa 10. They live in the home with their mother Shirley and their grandmother Lynn. Shirley has just finished preparing breakfast. She puts the food on the table. The kids all sit at the table in an orderly, almost military-like fashion. Shirley asked them if they brushed their teeth, washed up and made their beds. They all said yes ma'am, practically in unison.

"I guess your grandmother was tired because she's still sleeping," Shirley said as she briefly looked around for her. Jimmy reminded Shirley that grandma doesn't go to the recreation center until eleven. He pretty much kept up with things like that. "Oh, that's right. You all save her some breakfast... Jimmy would you bless the table?" Shirley said as she sat down at the table. Jimmy pauses, bows his head and says a short prayer. Everyone says amen and starts digging in.

The sound of knives and forks hitting plates fills the room. Lynn comes out and starts looking around. She wonders in the kitchen area. "Did you all save me some? It smells wonderful," she says as she tilts her head up to take a whiff. Shirley let her know there was plenty of food left over and asked her if she wanted her to fix her a plate. Lynn closes her housecoat and replies, "No, I am going to relax a little while longer. I just wanted to make sure you all saved me some breakfast." Lynn takes several slices of bacon from the pan and starts eating them like she's starving. She then grabs some more bacon, and everyone just looks at her surprised.

Lynn said, "This should be good for now. I'll be out in about an hour or so." Lynn turns around after practically inhaling the bacon and heads back to her bedroom. Everyone's eyes followed her, as she exited, because that was unusual behavior for Lynn. Shirley told Jimmy she wanted him, Larry and Will to clean up the yard today. Shirley always assigned chores for the boys and Jimmy, being the oldest, was in charge of making it happen. Jimmy was sort of like the man of the house. She advised them that Roy, their father who lived in the neighborhood, would probably have them all go over and touch up his yard at some point too. Jimmy let her know he had already planned on going over there with his brothers on Saturday.

PREDATOR ON THE DIAMOND: THE BOSTON RED SOX YOUTH MOLESTATION STORY

Shirley agreed with him and told him it was a good idea. "Lisa hurry up, so you don't miss the bus. You have about twenty minutes," Shirley said as she looked up on the clock on the wall and continued eating. Larry reminded Shirley he is supposed to go to the ballpark after school. "I know that Larry and Will is supposed to have basketball practice after school. You all still have to take care of your responsibilities around here!" Shirley said with a loud voice. Larry asked if it would be okay for them to do the yard tomorrow. "Okay, but I want it looking good. I want those rooms taken care of, the bathrooms cleaned, and the living room vacuumed. I want the kitchen taken care of too," she said authoritatively.

Larry let her know it would be taken care of. After all, if Shirley said something needed to get done, it got done with few questions asked. Since she was a single mother she had to be tough with them. Later on, that day, Will was picking up some items from a grocery store. He is there with his African American friend, Kevin. Kevin was slender and about one year younger than Will. As they are shopping they come across Fitzy. He walks up and leans on their shopping cart. He just leans there for a few seconds smiling at the two of them. Fitzy finally said, "Hey Kevin, how are you doing buddy?" Kevin told him he was doing okay.

Fitzy asked Kevin if he was coming out to the ballpark to work this season. Kevin had worked at the ballpark before. Kevin paused, looked at Will and then said, "Yes, I'll be out there." "That's great because we could sure use the help. How about you buddy, you interested in working at the ballpark?" Fitzy said as he focused his attention on Will. Will had never worked at the ballpark. His older brother Jimmy had worked there five years ago when he was fifteen and Will was ten. He brought Will to the ballpark on many occasions. Fitzy treated him like a son at the ballpark, at least as far as he remembered. Will let Fitzy know he was interested, but also let him know it would be up to his mother.

Fitzy said how wonderful it would be to have them work for him. "What's your name buddy?" He asked Will, still smiling. Will told Fitzy his full name. Fitzy squinted his eyes and looked up towards the ceiling for a second. The last name seemed familiar to Fitzy. "So, your last name is Jones, right? Well you can call me Mr. Fitzpatrick or Fitzy. I am the clubhouse manager for the Red Sox." Will asked Fitzy what he would need to do to work at the ballpark. He once again said he had to clear it with his mother. Deep inside Will knew his mother would be glad to see him doing something responsible. He would also get to work with his brother Larry.

PREDATOR ON THE DIAMOND: THE BOSTON RED SOX YOUTH MOLESTATION STORY

She was glad to send Jimmy out to the ballpark years ago. Will wanted to go back then, but Shirley felt he was too young, and would just be a burden on his older brother. "Well Kevin knows what you're supposed to do. Kevin, bring him down to the Hotel room tonight. We'll unload the equipment truck Saturday morning," Fitzy said. Kevin asked what time and Fitzy said, "Between eight and nine." "Is it the same room?" Kevin asked. Fitzy, once again with a smile, said, "Yeah buddy, same room on the second floor." Kevin told Fitzy they both would be there. Kevin did not sound or look too enthused about working at the park and Will wondered why. Will was very excited about it. "Okay I will see you two later," Fitzy said as he patted Will on his back.

Will said thanks to Fitzy and his excitement was quite notable. He would be working around major league baseball players as well as making money on the side. Fitzy walks away but looks back and smiles at them one final time. Will slaps Kevin five and said, "Yes! I'm going to be at the ballpark!" "Yeah that's cool," Kevin said nonchalantly. "What's the matter man? You look like you saw a ghost! Man, we are going to be working at the ballpark!" Will proclaimed proudly. "Hey, I said it's cool. I mean, it's okay, I guess," Kevin repeated, pretty much in the same tone. They both agreed to drop off the groceries and eat before they went over there.

Will planned on telling his mother about Fitzy's offer for him to work at the ballpark but wanted to wait. He never thought to tell her, Fitzy wanted to meet him and his friend at a hotel. If he had told her, she would have surely told him he could not go.

CHAPTER FOUR

At a Holiday Inn near Winter Haven, an illuminated sign reads, "Welcome Boston Red Sox." The parking lot is filled with cars. Will and Kevin had both rode their bikes to the hotel. Kevin is still rather quiet, and Will is still excited and upbeat. Later on, after Will and Kevin go into Fitzy's hotel room, Fitzy closes the blinds and the drapes. He then makes sure his door is locked and latched. "Hey, Will I'm really glad you could make it buddy. Have a seat and make yourself at home. You guys hungry?" Fitzy said happily, with one of his big smiles. Will and Kevin both said yes.

Fitzy pulls out a wad of cash. "Kevin why don't you run to McDonald's and get something for you and Will," Fitzy said as he gave Kevin some of the money. Kevin asked Will what he wanted. Will thought for a while and then said, "I want a big mac, large fries, a large coke and a hot apple pie." "Wow, you are a little hungry, huh buddy?" Fitzy said as he shook his head. Will did not get to eat dinner at home. His mother worked at night, so that was how he managed to be out so late.

She did not like him out passed ten, even on weekends. Kevin stuffs the money in his pocket. "Okay I'll be right back," Kevin says as he begins to unlatch the door and then leaves. Once again Fitzy makes sure the door is locked and latched. "How old are you buddy?" Fitzy asked Will. Will told Fitzy he was fifteen. Fitzy peaked out the blinds and then went over and turned on the radio. "Wow you are big and strong for your age buddy. First things first buddy. Have you ever had a physical?" Fitzy asked. Will told Fitzy he had not had a physical recently. Fitzy told Will he needed to have a physical before he could work at the ballpark in the morning.

He picked up the phone and said, "Let me check with the team doctor to see if he will let me take care of it tonight, because I would like you to start tomorrow." Fitzy punches some keys on the phone and at least appears to have contacted the doctor. In reality he is talking to a dial tone. Fitzy, still pretending to talk on the phone, says, "There is a young man here who needs a physical." This was not the first time Fitzy performed a physical on a clubby. He knew usually they were so excited to work at the park, they didn't mind him doing what he claimed was a physical. "Okay doc, I will take care of it tonight," Fitzy continued then hung up.

PREDATOR ON THE DIAMOND: THE BOSTON RED SOX YOUTH MOLESTATION STORY

"Okay buddy I got permission to give you the physical. Go ahead and take off your shirt," Fitzy continued. Will stands up and takes his shirt off. He appears to be nervous, but he did believe Fitzy had permission to do the physical, and that he knew what he was doing. "Yeah buddy you look good and strong. You need to be strong to be one of my clubbies," Fitzy reminded Will. He then asked Will to show him his muscles. Will flexes and shows his muscles. As Fitzy squeezed firmly on Will's muscles he told him they were not bad.

"What I really need to do right now is a strength test. I need you to put me in a headlock and squeeze as hard as you can," Fitzy said as he leaned forward to make his head accessible to Will. Will looks puzzled, but he does what he is told. Fitzy allows Will to put him in a headlock. Will's face becomes contorted as he appears to be squeezing and holding on for dear life. Fitzy, with somewhat of a muffled voice, says "Come on buddy squeeze! Squeeze as hard as you can buddy!" Will finally released him. Fitzy again told Will how strong he was. He proceeded to tell Will to drop his pants. Will looked a little more nervous and reluctant, but he does what he is told.

Fitzy told Will to just relax. For Fitzy, it was important to keep Will calm and relaxed. He needed to gain Will's trust completely. Fitzy stands right in front of Will and looks down. He grabs Will's genitals. "Okay, go ahead and cough buddy," Fitzy advises. Will starts to cough. Fitzy then says, "Whoa buddy that's real nice. Oh, you're real strong and healthy buddy." Will pulls away from Fitzy, pulls his pants up rather quickly, and sits in the chair. He fastens his pants and puts his shirt back on. Fitzy is startled and jumps back. He says, "Just relax buddy, it's okay. This is going to be our little secret. Nobody else needs to know about this physical."

There is a knock at the door. Fitzy first peaks through the blinds and then unlatches all the locks one by one. It's Kevin returning from McDonald's. He lets Kevin in and Kevin places the bags of food on the table. "Here's your change Fitzy." Fitzy told Kevin he could keep the change as long as he shared it with Will. Will gets up and walks up to Kevin. He whispers to Kevin telling him he was ready to go. "What about the food, you don't want to stay and eat?" Kevin whispered back. Will indicated he was ready to go now. Fitzy could hear their conversation and asked if they wanted to leave. "Yeah we need to get going," Will told Fitzy with a strong reply.

PREDATOR ON THE DIAMOND: THE BOSTON RED SOX YOUTH MOLESTATION STORY

Fitzy told Will, "I am finished here and you're good to go buddy. You're real strong buddy and I think you will make a fine clubby," Fitzy assured Will. Will unlatches all the locks and opens the door. Fitzy told the two of them he would see them tomorrow morning at the ballpark. Kevin ran over and snatched the food from the room table. Kevin says okay to Fitzy as Will practically drags Kevin along by his arm. "Come on Kevin I said let's just go," Will demanded. Kevin and Will walked their bikes down the hotel hallway to exit. "What's the matter Will? He did something to you, didn't he?" Kevin asked. Will looked at Kevin like he was crazy and said, "I don't want to talk about it. Just forget about it! Let's just get out of here!"

The next day, outside Will's home, Shirley is watering the lawn and her flowers. Fitzy pulls up, gets out of his car, and walks up to the house. Shirley stops watering the lawn to see what he wants. "Hey how are you doing Fitzy?" she asked waving her free hand as she still held the hose in her other. Fitzy told her he was fine. "I just came to ask you if it is alright for Will to come work at the ballpark. I can really use him," Fitzy said in a rather convincing tone. "That should be fine Fitzy if that's what he wants. His brother Larry already works out there, so now he will have his older brother out there with him."

Fitzy told Shirley how Larry is such a great kid. Shirley thanked him and asked, "So when can he start?" Fitzy said he actually was hoping he would show up this morning, but he didn't. He told her he could take him over to the ballpark right now. Shirley tells Fitzy to hold on one second, drops the hose, goes on the porch and yells Will's name through the screen door. Will comes to the door to see what Shirley wants. As he opens the screen door and steps outside, he looks shocked to see Fitzy standing out there. "Hey buddy you ready to go?" Fitzy asked with a big smile. Will said yes. He went back inside and grabbed a backpack. He came back outside and followed Fitzy to his car.

Will sat in the front passenger seat practically wedged against the door to avoid contact with Fitzy. He appeared to be extremely uncomfortable and nervous. As they drive down the road, Fitzy puts his right hand on the seat and starts to slowly move it towards Will as he keeps his left hand on the steering wheel to drive. "How come you didn't show up with Kevin at the ballpark this morning?" Fitzy asked. Will shrugs his shoulders saying he doesn't know. However, he did know why. Fitzy made him uncomfortable. He confused Will. He told Fitzy he needed to get permission from his mother first, which was actually true.

"So how are you doing buddy?" Fitzy asked as he slowly placed his hand on Will's thigh. Will jumps away, pushes Fitzy's hand away and gives him a mean look. "Take it easy buddy. It's going to be okay buddy. You're going to have a lot of fun at the ballpark. Yeah buddy a lot of fun. You just need to relax buddy, and everything will be fine," Fitzy said as he continues to try to gain Will's trust. Fitzy felt his persistence would eventually win Will over.

CHAPTER FIVE

At the Chain of Lakes Spring Training Facility, Fitzy is giving Will a tour of the facility. He is driving him around on the equipment cart. There are players working out and practicing. The players all greet Fitzy with, "Hey Fitzy" or "Hello Fitzy." Fitzy drives Will away from the main field and down towards the minor league fields. Fitzy stopped the cart and said, "See all that? You're with the big boys now buddy. You're going to be big time here buddy."

Fitzy once again puts his hand on Will's thigh and tries to rub it. Will pushes his hand away and tells him not to do that. "Take it easy buddy. Everything is okay buddy. I told you to just relax buddy. It's just me and you here now." Fitzy turns around and heads back to the main ballpark. There are several players carrying quite a bit of equipment and walking back towards the main ballpark. "Hey, Fitzy, can we put some of this on your cart?" one of the Caucasian players asked.

PREDATOR ON THE DIAMOND: THE BOSTON RED SOX YOUTH MOLESTATION STORY

Fitzy said it was no problem and he asked Will to help the guys with their equipment. Will jumps off the cart and helps the players put the equipment on the cart. "I'm telling you buddy; you're going to be big here. Don't worry; I will make sure you are taken care of here. You see, you're good and strong, so you are going to be just fine here," Fitzy said to Will with a smile, as he allowed Will to jump back in. Fitzy then drove the cart back to the main field. Will still looked very uncomfortable. The next afternoon, Fitzy's car could be seen rolling slowly through the neighborhood streets. He sees two young boys, who are brothers, walking down the street and he slowly cruises next to them.

Fitzy pulls over, honks his horn and gestures to the two boys to come over. The two boys go up to Fitzy's car. Their names are Darryl and Reggie. Darryl is a young thin black boy, about 10. Reggie is a stocky black boy about 12. "You boys still want to make some extra cash and get to meet some of the great baseball players?" Fitzy asked. "Yeah I do!" Darryl said as he jumped in front of Reggie, practically knocking him down. "What's your name again buddy? Is it Reggie?" Fitzy asked as he partially leaned out of the car window. Darryl abruptly corrected Fitzy and said, "No, I'm Darryl he is Reggie."

Fitzy asked them how they were doing, as he reached in his car and got some goodies. He handed the boys some candy and sodas. Darryl told Fitzy they were okay. Fitzy saw that Reggie was not speaking much, even though he was the oldest. "Wouldn't you like to work at the ballpark too?" Fitzy asked Reggie. Reggie said yes to Mr. Fitzpatrick with a sort of low, innocent voice. "Well let me see those muscles. You need to be strong to carry some of the equipment," Fitzy said as he put up his own arm to flex. Darryl and Reggie show their muscles. They practically give Fitzy a professional bodybuilding show with all their poses. Fitzy smiles and sits there for a little while watching them pose.

"Oh yeah, both of you guys are big and strong. So, do you guys think your parents will let you work for me?" Fitzy said, still smiling. Reggie told Fitzy their mother would be okay with it. "What about your father?" Fitzy asked. Reggie looks downward and gets quiet for a second. Darryl does the same thing. "We don't live with our father... He's in prison," Reggie said as he took a gulp of his soda. "That's good... I mean that's okay buddy. You two would be well taken care of buddy. You boys would be treated like family over there."

PREDATOR ON THE DIAMOND: THE BOSTON RED SOX YOUTH MOLESTATION STORY

Fitzy asked the boys if their mother was home right now. He wanted to have the opportunity to win over a parent once again. Fitzy was happy to find out Darryl and Reggie did not have a father. It was pretty easy for Fitzy to convince mothers to let their sons work at the ballpark. He made them feel he was instilling a sense of responsibility in their young boys. "Yes, our mother is home," Reggie said quickly. Fitzy, with a smile said, "Okay I will tell you what I can do. You two can hop in my car and I can take you home. I will personally talk to your mother." The two boys get into Fitzy's vehicle and Fitzy drives away. That evening Fitzy was in his hotel room.

He often spent evenings at the hotel. It was his favorite location to get more acquainted with the clubbies. Surprisingly, none of the guests at the hotel, which included Red Sox players, reported his actions. Fitzy was sitting in a comfortable room chair. He was relaxing and watching television. Ricky knocks on the door. Fitzy opens the door and Ricky walked in. "Hey Ricky, how are you doing buddy? Well come on in buddy," Fitzy said as he stepped aside to let Ricky by. Ricky said hello to Fitzy. Fitzy does his normal routine, which is to lock and latch the doors, make sure the blinds were closed and turn on the television or radio.

"Have a seat and make yourself at home buddy. You want a nice cold beer?" Fitzy said as he moved some clothing from a chair. Ricky looked around for a few seconds and said, "No thanks. I was just wondering if I could have some money." Fitzy told Ricky it was no problem. "Want to stay and spend a little time with me first?" Fitzy asked with a smile. Ricky quickly said no, and that he just needed to get some money. Fitzy starts loosening Ricky's belt, but Ricky pulls away and gives Fitzy a mean look. "Just take it easy buddy. It's okay buddy. It's just you and me buddy," Fitzy reminded Ricky as he attempted to calm him. Ricky, fixing his belt and pants says, "No I just want to go. I don't want to do this." Ricky starts unlocking the door to leave.

Fitzy goes up behind Ricky and holds the chain lock closed to prevent Ricky from unlocking it. He puts his free hand on Ricky's shoulder. "Come on buddy just stay for a little while," Fitzy said, almost pleading. "No, I said I just want to go!" Ricky yells. Fitzy gets his wallet off the dresser and takes about fifty dollars out. "Here you go buddy," Fitzy said as he hands Ricky the money. Ricky quickly took the money and thanked Fitzy. He told Fitzy he would visit him another time. Ricky unlatches the chain lock, opens the door and leaves. Fitzy is extremely angry. He slams the door and kicks a chair over. He felt teased in a way.

PREDATOR ON THE DIAMOND: THE BOSTON RED SOX YOUTH MOLESTATION STORY

This was certainly not the outcome he wanted. Usually, with money and gifts he was able to persuade these young boys. "That little son of a bitch! Damn him!" Fitzy said as he slams his fist down on the dresser and knocks over the bucket of ice. He then kicks the empty ice bucket. "Little ungrateful bastard!" Fitzy continued angrily. Fitzy picks up the empty ice bucket and heads out of the room to refill it with ice. After returning to his room with the ice, Fitzy places the filled ice bucket on the dresser. He is still visibly upset. There is a knock at the door. Fitzy answers the door. It's another young African American boy named Trevor. Trevor is short and about 16 years old. He has a notable bruise on his face.

Fitzy, looking closer at Trevor's face, asked "Hey Trevor how are you doing buddy?" "I'm okay Fitzy I was just coming to see if I could borrow your car," Trevor said as he looks downward. Fitzy lets Trevor in as he peaks back outside to make sure nobody is watching him. Fitzy closes the door and once again makes sure every lock is in place and secure on the door. He picks up the chair and the ice from the floor and tries to clean up the mess he made. "I made a little mess here, but I'll be right with you buddy. Sit down and make yourself at home. You want a beer buddy?" Fitzy said, continuing to tidy up the place.

Trevor thought about it for a minute, very cautiously. It was as if he knew what Fitzy's plan was. Still, reluctantly, Trevor said yes. Fitzy, with his usual smile, said "Go ahead and grab one from the fridge. They should be nice and cold for you buddy." Fitzy often kept alcohol, usually cold beers, in his refrigerator for the young boys. Trevor grabs a beer from the fridge, sits on the bed and downs the beer like water. "That was pretty good huh buddy?" Fitzy asked. Trevor acknowledged that it was good, and Fitzy asked him if he wanted another one. Trevor, once again giving it some thought, said he would have another one. Trevor gets up to get another beer. "No, you just relax buddy I will get it," Fitzy offered.

Fitzy brings out two more beers. Seeing how fast he drank the first one he felt it only made sense to have two waiting. Once again, Trevor slams them down like water. "You were a little thirsty huh buddy?" Fitzy asked with somewhat of a giggle. "Yeah," Trevor said sort of nonchalantly, as he appeared to be getting sleepy. "That's it for you buddy. I don't want you to wreck my car," Fitzy said as he collected the now empty beer bottles. "It's okay, I'm cool now," Trevor said as he lied back, putting his hands behind his head. "You want to hear some music or some-thing buddy?" Fitzy asked. Trevor said he was okay but was just feeling sleepy. Fitzy said, "Well you can lie down and make yourself comfortable buddy."

PREDATOR ON THE DIAMOND: THE BOSTON RED SOX YOUTH MOLESTATION STORY

"I know what you are going through at home. I am just here to help you buddy. Believe me, I won't hit you like him," Fitzy continued. Trevor continues to lie on the bed for a minute, but then falls asleep. Moments later, when Trevor wakes up, Fitzy is on his knees watching him. Trevor's pants are open. Trevor quickly jumps up off the bed and fastens his pants. Hey buddy it's okay. "Oh, my goodness, you're a big feller! Oh yeah you are going to be my number one clubby for sure. I will make sure the players and everyone in the Red Sox organization takes good care of you and your family. You are going to be the big man in the clubhouse," Fitzy said with excitement.

Trevor zips and buckles his trousers. He looks emotionless, like he is in a state of shock. He puts his head down and walks towards the door. Fitzy, suddenly disappointed, says "Hey little buddy don't you want the car keys?" Trevor does not answer. He just stands there with his head down as if he is ashamed. Fitzy walks up and puts the keys in Trevor's pocket. "Here buddy take these. That's what you came for right?" Fitzy said. Fitzy takes out a crisp one-hundred-dollar bill and puts it in Trevor's hand. "That should help you out a little buddy. I have to take care of you buddy. Oh man, you're going to be my best clubby," Fitzy said as he began to massage Trevor's shoulders.

Trevor unlocks all the locks and latches, turns around and gives Fitzy one more look. "Drive carefully buddy, I wouldn't want to see my number one clubby get hurt," Fitzy said with a smile and a wink. Trevor just put his head down again and walked out of the room. Fitzy stood there watching him for a while and shaking his head. Later that evening, Fitzy had fallen asleep with the lamp and television on. He is clearly having a recurring nightmare as he twists and turns wildly. Fitzy is in his childhood home. He is about seven years old. He runs into his room closet. He does not have clothes on. The faint sound of him crying and breathing heavily can be heard.

Fitzy peaks through the closet doors and sees a man looking under the bed for him. The man is Caucasian with a medium build. The man gets up, walks towards the closet and snatches the doors open. Fitzy looks up at the man like he has seen the devil himself. Fitzy is crying and has noticeable bruises on his face. The man is only wearing a towel. The man stands there with his hands on his hips shaking his head as he looks down on little Fitzy. He bends down and snatches Fitzy. Fitzy wakes up and sits up in his bed abruptly like a zombie awakening from the dead. He sits at the side of his bed. He is sweating profusely. Fitzy throws the remote control and one of his pillows. He takes a washcloth, dips it into the ice bucket and pats his face and neck.

CHAPTER SIX

It is the early morning at Michelle's home. Michelle is sitting on the couch. She looks at her watch several times and appears to be growing anxious. She picks up the phone and starts dialing. "Hello, my name is Michelle Mills, and I would like to report my son as missing…Well he has always been home by this time, especially on school nights…What do you mean it's not really an emergency? It's an emergency to me! Fine, I'll dial your damn non-emergency number!" Michelle says to the officer. As Michelle begins to dial again, Ricky comes through the door.

Michelle hangs up and just stares at Ricky with a mean look. "Where the hell have you been boy? And you better not lie to me!" Michelle yelled. Ricky just stands there with his head down and does not respond. Michelle jumps off the couch angrily and said, "Boy don't make me come over there! I asked you where you have been. It's twelve-thirty in the morning!" "Momma I'm sleepy, can I just go to bed?" Ricky asked. Michelle just looked at Ricky and said with a squint in her eyes, "No you can't! Now sit your ass down."

"You had me worried half to death!" She continued. Ricky sits down with his head still down and plays with his hands nervously. Michelle slowly approaches Ricky as if she is going to attack. She stands right in front of him and says, "Now I am going to ask you one more time, where have you been?" Ricky told her he was with Mr. Fitzpatrick at first and then he went over his friend's house for a while. Michelle, poking Ricky in the head, says "You are supposed to be in your damn bed sleeping not running the streets. Now I want to know what your problem is." "Momma I don't have a problem," Ricky says as tears begin to well up in his eyes.

Michelle crosses her arms in front of her. Ricky's tears do not impress her. She felt Ricky was just being overly dramatic. "Oh yes you do Ricky. Your grades are dropping, you're getting in trouble in school, and you're not doing what you are supposed to around here. Basically, you are doing whatever you want around here!" Michelle said, still angry. "Momma I don't feel like talking about it right now," Ricky said with a low voice. He sort of jumped back expecting a slap, which he never received. "Ricky! Now you are testing my patience! Now, we can stay down here all night if that's what you want, but you are going to tell me what's wrong with you," Michelle demanded.

Ricky began to fidget more aggressively, and the tears began to flow down his face. "Mr. Fitzpatrick touched me," he finally blurted out. Michelle still looked puzzled. It took her a few seconds to digest what she had just heard. "What do you mean he touched you? Touched you how?" Michelle inquires. Ricky told her Mr. Fitzpatrick touched him on his private parts. Michelle stood over him with her hands on her hips and her mouth wide open. She was really speechless at this point.

It was not unusual for Ricky to tell stories. He was also somewhat of the practical joker and actor of the family. In fact, there were even times when Ricky could cry on cue to avoid a spanking. "Ricky I am tired of your lies! Fitzy would never do anything like that to you. Your lies are going to cause someone to get in some serious trouble. Don't you dare say something like that about him when he has been out there constantly trying to help you boys in this neighborhood. He has been doing that for years," Michelle said. Ricky tried his best to convince his mother he is telling the truth. However, Michelle cut him off and told him she did not want to hear it. She even hit him upside his head once or twice.

"Now go to bed before I do something I don't want to do to you. And don't be surprised if you are grown before you get off punishment!" Michelle said as she pointed towards the stairs. Ricky walked away crying with his head down. He was truly crushed that his mother did not believe him. "Lord have mercy. I don't know what has gotten into that boy. I sure hope he doesn't end up like his father," Michelle said shaking her head in disgust.

CHAPTER SEVEN

At a high school basketball game hundreds of visitors and guests cheer for their team. The scoreboard reads, Visitors 48 and Home 46. There are eight seconds left in the game. Will was on the home team and was actually a good player. He is a school and crowd favorite. The chant from the crowd is quite loud and is, "Will! Will! Will!" Will dribbles down the court threading his way through the defense. Will takes a long-range jumper just as the final buzzer sounds.

Will hit a three-point shot and there is a roar and celebration in the audience as people stand, cheer, and give each other high fives. Coach Sanders, a Caucasian man, and the rest of the team run out to celebrate with Will and the players on the floor. They all surround Will, pump their fists and chant: "Will! Will! Will!" "Will you made another tough shot and saved us again!" Coach Sanders said as he patted will on the back. Many of the friends and fans come over to celebrate and basically let the team know they are loved.

The next day, at the high school, the final bell indicating the end of the school day sounds. The hallway suddenly fills with students. Will walks down the hall with Jan and Kathy, two Caucasian females 16 years old. Will was quite popular with the young ladies at the high school; both Caucasian and African American. However, he tended to prefer Caucasian females. His two best friends Troy, white, 14 and Brad, black, 14 were also there. "Damn Will, you are the man!" Troy said. Brad pumped his fist up and said, "Yeah, Will but that was your shot. You never miss that shot man," Troy proudly said, "Will almost never misses, period."

Troy asked Will if he was going up to "The Point" tonight to hang with some of the folks. "The Point" was near a wooded area, not far from Will's house. It was a place many of the high school students liked to hang out. Some would smoke, some would drink, and some even did drugs there. For the most part it was a private place for them to go to get away from the rules of adults. "I don't know, maybe," Will said with uncertainty. Most of the time, it depended on whether his mother was at home or at work that night. His mother worked nights most of the time, but once in a while she would have a night off. His older brother would tend to look the other way and allow Will to stay out late.

Will, after pondering the question a little longer, said, "Yeah I will probably go." "Come on Will, we have more fun when you go. Shit if you don't go, there won't be any chicks," Brad said with a big smile. Jan shook her head and said, "Brad, chicks? You're such an asshole!" "Oh, I am sorry Jan, I mean beautiful young ladies. By the way, are you ladies coming out?" Brad inquired, hoping for a positive response. Kathy laughed and said, "Not if you go Brad... No, I am just kidding; we will go if Will goes."

Brad once again confirmed Will was going. "Shoot all he has to do is walk a short distance from his house," Brad said. "So, are you going Will? Let us know right now because we need to get ready," Pat said as she paused for Will's response. Will, still looking confused, finally said "Okay, okay I will be there!" Brad began to jump up and down in celebration like a small child. Kathy asked, "What time should we be there?" Will answered and told her about eight or so. "Okay we will see you guys then," Kathy agreed. As the girls walked away to go to their respective classes, Brad reminded them to bring some of their girlfriends. Troy reluctantly agreed to go along also. Ironically, Troy preferred to hang with the black girls.

Later on, that evening, at "The Point," a couple of cars drive up a dirt road to a large oak tree in an open wooded area near Will's home. It's several of Will's Caucasian friends including Brad and Troy. On the other side of the dirt road, on a lit-up porch, older black men play cards, drink, joke, laugh and talk. They keep a watchful eye on the young teenagers. They generally ignored the teens, and the teens did not bother them either. "Where the hell is Will? We should walk over to his house and knock on his door," Brad said as he looked around. "Trust me, if Will said he would be here he will be here," Troy replied.

A beautiful Silver Mercedes pulls up. Kathy, Pat and Jan are inside. Pat is Caucasian, about 16. Jan is driving and lets down her window. "Where is Will?" Jan asked. "Will should be here soon. Just hold on for a little while," Brad said with just a little doubt. Jan said they would wait there a while for him, but that it would just be for a while. Brad said, "Hey, we got a cooler in the trunk with some beers in it if you guys want a beer." "We'll wait for Will right now. We will probably have one when he gets here," Jan said as she rolled her window back up. The girls drive up and park under the large tree.

PREDATOR ON THE DIAMOND: THE BOSTON RED SOX YOUTH MOLESTATION STORY

"Shit, Will better show up or I am going to personally kill him!" Brad said as he popped open a beer. Four more of Will's Caucasian friends, Michael, Tim, Frank and Mark, all 15, pull up in a nice car. Will does show up as promised. He walks through the woods and up to the dirt road where "The Point" is. He walks up to Troy and Brad's car to greet them. "I told you Will would show up," Troy said with a sigh of relief. He continued saying, "Hey Will what's up? You had me worried for a minute man." Will, after slapping everyone five said, "I had a few things I needed to take care of, but hey, I made it like I promised." Jan, Kathy and Pat get out of their car and go over to where Will is.

One by one they give Will a hug. Kathy said, "Hello Will, we're glad you made it out." Brad goes over, gets a large cooler and sets it down. "Okay everyone we have some cold brews here!" Brad shouted proudly. "Will gets the first one!" Troy shouted just as loud. "Hey, I am cool with that," Brad said as he tossed one to Will. "Damn Will, you are definitely the man! It looks like we are going to have a party tonight!" Michael said with contentment. Will just smiles, nods and winks. He reaches in one of the cars and turns the music up as they all begin to mingle and drink.

The next afternoon, Will was at the Winter Haven facility clubhouse getting some of the equipment ready for the players. An African American baseball player, Charles, confronts Will. "Will, I need to talk to you," he said as he led Will to a more private area. "What's up?" Will asked with a surprised look on his face. In fact, he looked a little frightened. Looking around to make sure the coast was clear; Charles said, "I have a question to ask you." "What do you need to know?" Will asked. Charles, looking around again, asked, "Is Fitzy Gay?" Will stands there surprised for a few seconds. He needs those few seconds to recover from the question. "I... I... Umm I don't know," Will nervously replied.

Charles sort of walks away briefly to compose himself. He could tell Will was lying. He walks back up to Will, looks him right in the eyes and says, "Look at me man!" Will slowly and reluctantly looks at him. "Don't you lie to me boy! Is Fitzy gay?" He repeated the question. Will puts his head down. Embarrassed, he said, "Yeah he's gay." Charles appeared to be real upset as he said, "I knew it! Does he try anything with you guys? Be honest." "Yeah, he touches us, and he likes to try to put his mouth on us," Will reluctantly answered. "Thanks for telling me Will. Have you told anyone else about that fucking asshole?" Charles asked. Will said, "No you're the only one I told."

Charles looked around again and said, "Good, don't discuss it with anyone. I am going to make sure this gets taken care of. Trust me, it will be taken care of. You just try to stay away from that cat man," Charles warned. Charles did not intend to turn Fitzy in, but he wanted Will to believe that he did. Many of the players knew Fitzy liked the young boys known as clubbies. There were even jokes inside the locker room amongst the players about Fitzy liking "those young black boys." They were known as "Fitzy's Boys." Nobody ever stepped in to stop it.

In fact, most of them turned the other way, because Fitzy was well-known and well-liked. "Is there anything else you want to talk to me about? I mean is everything else okay?" Charles asked. Will said everything else was cool as he turned to walk away. "Well Will, you know I'll look out for you, so if you have a problem just let me know. But don't go to anyone else." Charles assured Will. He continued, "In fact you tell all the clubbies to come to me or one of the other players if they have a problem with Fitzy," Charles said. "Okay I will," Will responded. Charles walks up to Will, puts out his hand and Will slaps it five. Will goes and finishes up what he was doing.

CHAPTER EIGHT

At the Chain of Lakes ballpark, it is in the late afternoon and the Red Sox have a game. It is the last out and thousands of fans head towards the exits. The announcer's voice can be heard in the background calling the play-by-play. Moments later, at the visitor's clubhouse, Fitzy has all his clubbies preparing the clubhouse for the players. While they are working Fitzy decides to give them a pep talk. "Okay now that was a hell of a game. Now it's time for us to get back down to business. We are real good at this now so it shouldn't take us all night," Fitzy said with his usual smile.

One of the clubbies raises his hand to talk to Fitzy. Fitzy continued, "I'll get to you in a minute. What I wanted to say is that you guys are doing an excellent job. You all have been keeping up with the needs of the players and that keeps them happy, so it keeps me happy too. Any one of you can be in my position someday. I started out here as a clubby just like you guys. Having said all of that, let's continue getting ready for the players. Kevin, I can answer your question after everything is ready. Okay let's get going!"

PREDATOR ON THE DIAMOND: THE BOSTON RED SOX YOUTH MOLESTATION STORY

The home-side clubhouse is run by Tony. Tony is a middle-aged Caucasian man. He shows up on the visitor's side where Will is working with several other clubbies. "Okay Mark, I am going to leave you in charge of the visitor's clubhouse this afternoon. Make sure everything gets cleaned, loaded or stowed properly. Will, I need to talk to you in private. Tony takes Will to another clubhouse room and slams the door.

Tony makes sure the door is secure as he latches it. "Remember what we discussed. There is to be no more talk about Fitzy being gay, a fag or touching you guys around here. You were put on the visitor's side because Fitzy felt you were a good clubby. If I hear another player, clubby or anyone else tell me you said something like that about Fitzy you will be out of here on your head! Understood?" Will is silent for a few seconds.

He is surprised and shocked that he is being reprimanded this way. Moreover, he did not expect the conversation he had with Charles to get back to Tony. "Yes I understand," Will replied. "Now I'm telling you this, but it comes straight from the top. Do you understand that young man?" Tony said with a certain urgency in his voice. Will, with a low innocent voice said, "Yeah I got it." Tony wanted to make sure things were clear with Will. "Now go to the home side! You will be working with me for a while."

"Now I believe you have a lot of potential and can go a long way here just like Fitzy said. But you need to keep your mouth shut and do what you're told. Now get in there with the other clubbies." Will leaves, but he is visibly upset. He heads outside to get some fresh air and calm down. Will is outside on the baseball field. There are still people in the stands. A Caucasian gentleman, Ron, and his son Pete were down in the front row. "Excuse me young man, can I talk to you a second?" Ron said politely.

Will began to look around because he did not believe this fan was talking to him. Will assumed the fan was talking to him because there was nobody else around, but he did say, "Who me?" Ron replied. "Yes you, please come here for a second." Will does what he is told. He walks up to Ron and his son and said, "Yes sir." Ron asked Will if he and his son could have his autograph. Will was clearly speechless. He had never had anyone ask for his autograph since he worked at the park up to that point. "You want my autograph?" Will asked again to make sure he heard correctly. Ron told Will his son wanted his autograph. Will searched his pocket for a pen. Ron handed Will a pen and a Boston Red Sox ball cap. "You can sign it right under the bill," Ron said.

PREDATOR ON THE DIAMOND: THE BOSTON RED SOX YOUTH MOLESTATION STORY

"What's your son's name?" Will inquired. "His name is Peter, but you can make it to Ron and Peter." Will scribbles down his autograph and hands the ball cap to Peter. Peter's eyes light up with satisfaction. "What do you say Peter?" Ron asked. "Thank you," Peter quickly said. Ron shook Will's hand and told him they appreciated what he did. They then walked away. Will watched Fitzy drive up to the stands past him with the equipment cart. He always carried his bag of goodies with him, even as he drove the cart.

He lifts a young African American boy from the front row and puts him on the cart as his mother and father smile and wave to their little son. Fitzy drives off towards the unoccupied lower fields. His cart disappears as they go out of sight. Will watches, shakes his head and walks away. "Damn! If they knew where he was taking him and what he's going to do to him they wouldn't be smiling and waving," Will said disappointed. It was not unusual for Fitzy to drive young boys away from the main fields to do what he wanted with them. He was quite bold at this point, because he still was not considered a threat to the boys.

CHAPTER NINE

The next week Will was sweeping out and cleaning the Umpire's room in the clubhouse. He was now back on the visitor's side. Fitzy came in the door and closed it behind himself. Fitzy slowly approaches Will. "Hello buddy. I haven't heard from you in a while buddy. You are still my number one clubby and I don't have any hard feelings for you." Will starts backing up slowly. Fitzy continues, "Come on buddy just relax." Will backed up to a wall where he could not go any further. "I just want to go," Will said.

Fitzy was not willing to let Will leave so easily. Fitzy believed he needed to be somewhat aggressive with Will. "Look buddy it's just you and me. Just relax buddy. Nobody else needs to know what I do to you. It's our little secret. There is no need for you to go telling folks about us. It's none of their business. Now I don't expect you to talk to anyone else about me. If you do, it may not be pleasant for you around here. I mean, I am just letting you know."

PREDATOR ON THE DIAMOND: THE BOSTON RED SOX YOUTH MOLESTATION STORY

Will starts walking towards Fitzy so he can bypass him and get to the door. "Excuse me," Will said, almost in a pleading tone. Fitzy catches up to Will and quickly bypasses him. He then stands in front of the door and asks, "Where you going so fast buddy? Don't you want to finish cleaning up buddy?" Will stood there for a few seconds to analyze the situation. Fitzy was putting him in a position of few choices. He wondered if Fitzy would force him to fight his way out of there. Will even looked at the broom he was still holding in his hand.

"No, I just want to leave!" Will said with more conviction. Fitzy is startled and jumps a bit. Fitzy said, "Well can I just watch you work buddy? I kind of miss you since you went over to the other side for several days. You know those folks on that side aren't going to take care of you like I will buddy. I take care of all you guys." Will just shrugs his shoulders as if he did not care. "Can I go now?" Will asked. Fitzy, still standing in front of the door, says "Do you realize that there are no colored boys on the home side in Boston? The visitor's side has colored boys. I am the only one who is going to take care of you guys in this organization. No one else is going to take care of you guys like me." Will leaves rather quickly after Fitzy does finally step aside.

Fitzy looks visibly upset and just stands there, shaking his head as he yelled, "That little son of a bitch! After all I have done for him." Later that evening, Will pulls up to his house. He gets out of one of the player's vehicle and is approached by two boys who ride up to him on their bicycles. Emmitt is a black boy around 12 and Jerry was a black boy around 13. "Wow! Will whose car is this?" Jerry asked. Will leans on the car and with a big smile says, "It's my car." "Come on Will stop lying that ain't your car," Emmitt challenged Will.

"Actually, it belongs to one of the baseball players," Will finally admitted, still smiling. "He's letting you drive his car?" Jerry asked. "Yeah he is letting me take care of it for a little while. I have to take it to get washed and stuff," Will replied. Jerry asked if he and Emmitt could go, but Will told him it would not be a good idea. Jerry, looking disappointed, said "Man you guys get cars, cash and everything for working at the ballpark. Shoot all we got is these stupid bicycles." "Yeah and you guys get to meet all the baseball players," Emmitt added. "I can't wait until next season," Jerry said. Will, now curious, asked "Why? What happens next season?" "We're going to be working at the park next season," Emmitt bragged.

PREDATOR ON THE DIAMOND: THE BOSTON RED SOX YOUTH MOLESTATION STORY

This was certainly not good news to Will. He did not want any more of the young boys in the neighborhood to go through what he was going through. "You guys sure you want to do that? I mean it's a lot of hard work." "Yeah we're sure," Jerry proclaimed. Will looks at the guys, shakes his head and walks away. He stops in his tracks and turns around once again. He says, "You guys think being a clubby is so great, but you don't even know what you're getting into." Will then walked away. The two boys look at each other with a puzzled look. "What the hell is his problem?" Emmitt asked. "I don't know. He's just mad because we're going to be doing what he's doing. They all just want to keep everything to themselves," Jerry said. "Yeah, let's just forget about him. He ain't nobody," Jerry continued as they both rode away on their bikes.

CHAPTER TEN

Several days later Will was inside his house. He stands in the doorway a minute to look at some exotic plants sitting in the living room. Shirley always had beautiful plants. She even maintained a garden outside the house. He walks in the Kitchen where Shirley and his grandmother, Lynn are. Lynn is sitting at the dining room table and Shirley is finishing up cooking the meal. "Hey Will," Shirley said. Will hugged her and said, "Hi momma. Those are some nice plants are you going to keep them in here?"

"No, I just put them in here for a while," Shirley replied. Will hugs Lynn and says hello to her. He opened the pot and said, "That smells good. I just wanted to grab a plate, eat and head back out." Shirley just looked at Will with that motherly look for a few seconds. Being a single parent had made her somewhat protective. Even though she had to work in the evenings and Will's older brother and grandmother was there, she still wanted to be aware of Will's activities.

"Okay, but what time do you plan on being back?" Shirley asked. Will sat at the table and replied, "I should be back around nine or so." "You know you have school in the morning, so don't be fooling around out there. And don't be in every grownup's face you see either. You don't need to be around all them grown folks. You're a child and you should stay in a child's place," Shirley warned. Will just sighed, leaned back in his seat and said, "I am usually just around the baseball players." "Well, that's fine, but you need to do your job and get on out of there. You don't need to be socializing and hanging out with them," Shirley once again advised. Will agreed to do what his mother said.

He really just wanted her to acknowledge he was doing positive things. He also wanted her to treat him like a young man who is responsible. He never felt like she was proud of him. Fact of the matter is she had to be tough on him. She wanted him to be a productive man. "Who does that car belong to?" Shirley asked as she put the dinner on the table. Will looked at his grandmother first, and then Shirley who was now standing over him. "It belongs to one of the baseball players. I just was getting it washed for him," Will answered. Shirley did not like what she was hearing. She Knew Will was not a driver yet. "Well, you just be careful driving all over the place with those fast cars," she said as she sat down at the table.

Shirley asked, "How come you and Larry don't come home together? I mean since you both work at the ballpark." Will said he did not know why but believed Fitzy would bring him home. Larry, as if on cue, came in. As he makes eye contact with Will, he puts his head down and then looks away. Will just shakes his head. He bows his head to say a silent prayer and then starts helping himself to the food. Larry and Will were both experiencing some of the same things at the ballpark, but they dare not tell Shirley. "Hello Larry," Shirley said. Larry just stands there with his head still down for a while. He finally acknowledges Shirley and says hello.

Larry goes into the kitchen and loads some food on his plate. He is clearly upset, as he often was, coming from the ballpark. As Larry sat down, Will got up and said, "I'm not hungry anymore." Shirley watched Will walk away. She knew there had to really be something going on for Will to walk away from food. "Larry you need to tell me what's going on. You two have been acting funny lately. Will doesn't ever walk away from food, and you just come in here with the silent treatment every evening." Larry responded by saying, "It's nothing, momma. We are just tired when we come from the ballpark. It ain't easy being clubby." Shirley throws her hands up with discontent. She does not like being kept in the dark. "Fine, you two just go on about your business!"

CHAPTER ELEVEN

Inside the clubhouse showers, several of the clubbies are taking a shower, including Will. It's an open shower area that the players use. It was not unusual for the clubbies to utilize the showers. They had permission to take showers, as long as the players were not around, or needing to use them. Fitzy walks up with a hand full of towels.

He stands right at the shower entrance and watches the boys shower. "Hello, my buddies; I got your towels right here. I'll take care of you. Don't mind me just keep on showering. There is no rush, so you guys can take as much time as you want. Whoa buddy, this is the best view in the house! Let me see those muscles!"

One by one the clubbies leave the shower as they put on their underwear. Fitzy slowly hands each one of them a towel after giving them a complete head-to-toe evaluation and kissing their chests. Will is the last clubby left in the shower because he needs to rinse the soap off himself. Will walks over to Fitzy to get a towel.

Will has his hands over his private area to shield himself from Fitzy. "Hey buddy, it looks like it's just you and me here now. Here's your towel buddy." Will reaches for the towel, but Fitzy pulls it back from him. "Not so fast buddy, just relax buddy," Fitzy said. Will was in a very bad and vulnerable position. He needed that towel, but he would be just as content to walk home naked or with his clothes soaked and wet if he had to. "Can I get a towel please?" Will asked kindly. Fitzy holds the towel out once again and Will snatches it. He walks away mumbling and shaking his head as he wraps the towel around himself.

Fitzy just laughs and smacks Will on the butt with his hand as he passes by. "You're still my number one clubby Will. Boy are you ever my number one clubby. You and I are going to do some big things together. You just listen to me, and I will make sure you're taken care of." There was a Caucasian player who witnessed Fitzy's actions with Will. He just turned around and walked back out. The next day, several of the baseball field groundskeepers were working on the baseball field. There are also two young black boys, who were running around and playing. Mark is six and Terrance is ten years old. Fitzy drives up in the equipment cart with a big smile on his face. "Hey how are you guys doing?" Fitzy asked the groundskeepers.

PREDATOR ON THE DIAMOND: THE BOSTON RED SOX YOUTH MOLESTATION STORY

The groundskeeper, who is the father of the two boys, Mike, said, "Okay, how about you Fitzy?" "Oh, I can't complain. You guys are really making the field look good and kept up," Fitzy responded. Terrance and Mark run up to Mike. They ask to play up in the stands, but Mike tells them to stay where he can see them. Mark runs up to Fitzy's cart and gets on it. There were many times when the groundskeepers let Fitzy watch their sons. They too trusted Fitzy and for some reason felt he offered something positive to them. "Hey little buddy, how are you doing?" Fitzy asked.

Mark told Fitzy he was doing fine. His brother Terrance kept his distance from Fitzy. He seemed to sense there was something not right with Fitzy. "Why don't you let them work for me? They look like they're good and strong, and I'm pretty sure they could handle the job," Fitzy said. The boys go running down the field. Mike just laughed and said, "Fitzy, now you're good with these young boys around here and I would even go so far as to say you have a way with them. But my boys are quite a handful. You see I like you Fitzy and I wouldn't do that to you. I think of you as a friend, and I would like to keep it that way."

Fitzy smiled even more so and said, "That might be true, but most of the guys I have working for me used to have some serious disciplinary problems. Right now, they are some of my best clubbies. I mean most of these young men come from some pretty rough backgrounds." "Then maybe we should be asking you how you do it," Mike said inquisitively. Realistically, Mike felt his boys were way too young to work at the park. However, this had never stopped Fitzy from getting to even younger boys than them in the past. Fitzy was only discussing it because he really did hope to have the boys work there at the park at some capacity.

"I guess a lot of them just need a strong male figure in their lives. Many of them are from single parent homes, usually without a father. I just establish trust with them first," Fitzy said, revealing his strategy. Mike was all ears now and wanted to hear more. He leaned against the cart and asked, "Do you feel you can do that with any young child?" Fitzy confidently said, "Yeah, I believe so. I have been at it for quite a while." Mike sort of chuckled and said, "So, maybe I should bring my daughters out here to you. That is if you can have the same effect on young girls."

PREDATOR ON THE DIAMOND: THE BOSTON RED SOX YOUTH MOLESTATION STORY

Fitzy would never have girls working for him at the ballpark. He knew Mike was joking about females being in the clubhouse "Unfortunately, I can't hire female clubbies. You notice there are no female clubbies around here. Number one, the job requires the clubbies to go in and out of the men's locker rooms and bathrooms. Number two, the league would never go for it," Fitzy said almost with a contented voice. Mike smiled, looked around and said, "Yeah I know all that Fitzy, but who knows, maybe someday that will change."

"I don't know, maybe, but I doubt it," Fitzy replied. "You don't get off that easy Fitzy. I'm about ready to bring all my nephews to you. Shit that would definitely be a test for you," Mike said as he smiled back at Fitzy. Fitzy said, "Bring them here if you want. The only requirement is that they have to be somewhat strong. The job can sometimes be physically challenging," Fitzy remarked. Fitzy asked to take the young boys for a ride on the cart. He wanted to get them away from their father for a while. Mike was more than happy to take a break from his two sons and told Fitzy it would be fine.

"Now the one with the blue shirt is Terrance and the one in the white shirt is Mark. Feel free to keep them," Mike told Fitzy jokingly. Fitzy gets on the cart and says, "Who wants to go for a ride?" Mark and Terrance both run up to the cart. "Okay I can take one of you at a time. Who is going to be first?" Fitzy asked as he wanted to isolate them.

Mark practically knocked his brother down saying, "Me first! Me first!" Fitzy drives off with Mark. The groundskeepers continue working on the baseball field. Mike said, "That poor man will never be the same. Watch out, because he'll probably be tearing up the field with that cart to get him back here." They all get a laugh as they watch Mark and Fitzy ride through the baseball field. Unfortunately, they were completely unaware of his true intentions.

CHAPTER TWELVE

It is a starlit evening. Will and two other black clubbies are with a couple of the baseball players at a night spot. One of the players, Dan, is a Caucasian male. The other player, Bob, is also a Caucasian Male. As Will and the other clubbies step up to the entrance a rather large black security guard holds up his hand. "Do you young men have some identification cards for me to see?" The security guard asked. "Oh, these guys are with us. We play for the Boston Red Sox and these guys work for us," Bob said as he stepped forward.

The security guard looked at the young clubbies for a second or two. He knew they were under-aged for the club. However, these guys they were with were from the Boston Red Sox. "Okay, no problem man. You guys come right on in. The Boston Red Sox are in here tonight!" The security guard said as he let them all by and slapped the two players five. The guys all go up to an open table and have a seat. The two players take off their Boston Red sox ball caps and jackets. "Okay Will, what do you guys want?" Dan asked.

Will looked around for a second. The question was clear, but Will was not so sure he wanted everyone around to know his answer. After all they were minors in an adult establishment. "Can we have some beer?" The two players looked at each other for a second and started laughing. Will looked puzzled as he did not know what to make of their laughter. "These boys want some beers," Dan said as he continued to laugh. "What kind of beer?" Bob asked. Will, surprised at the question said, "We like Michelob." The player raised his hand, and the waitress came over.

The waitress, a Caucasian female, asked "How can I help you gentlemen?" "Bring them each a Michelob and bring two bottles of Champagne," Dan said. The clubbies just continued to look at each other and to look around. They appeared to be nervous. None of them had ever been in a club before. However, other clubbies had gone with players to night spots before. Bob said, "Well you guys have been doing a great job at the clubhouse and I mean that. You guys have really been taking care of us. Tonight, we are going to take care of you guys." The clubbies all thanked the players as the waitress brought back the drinks.

PREDATOR ON THE DIAMOND: THE BOSTON RED SOX YOUTH MOLESTATION STORY

Two very attractive Caucasian females walk past the table. Will's mouth drops as he watches them walk to the bar. He looks to be in a trance-like state. Dan waved his hand in Will's face to get his attention and yells, "Will!" Will does not budge. Bob claps his hands right in front of Will's face and does get his attention as Will jumps. The two players start laughing hysterically. "Will, you wouldn't even know what to do with them," Dan said. Will just smiled and took a swig of beer. "Yeah you are a basketball star at your high school, and yeah you have a lot of young white ladies hanging all over you there. However, those two ladies, I say again ladies, are not in high school. They're way out of your league," Bob said.

Will just continued to laugh. Dan slaps a one-hundred-dollar bill on the table and said, "This hundred-dollar bill says you can't get a number from either one of them." Will and the other clubbies looked at the hundred-dollar bill and then looked at the two players. Everyone then focuses their attention on Will. "Sounds like a good bet to me Will," Bob acknowledged. Will leaves the table and walks up to the girls. He is talking to them, but their conversation is not audible. He points to the table where the baseball players are. He gets a napkin and ink pen from the bar.

He writes on the napkin, walks back to the table, slams down the napkin and snatches the hundred-dollar bill. When Will sat down, he was treated like he was the man. The players and the clubbies all patted him on the back and slapped him five. Will told the players the two females would be joining them at the table. The two players paused and looked at each other. They realized what Will had done. "Will, I know exactly how you got their numbers. You told them who we are!" Will started to laugh and said, "Hey, you didn't say how I had to get the numbers, right?" Dan, somewhat embarrassed, said, "Okay you got that one over on me. Damn it Will, you are slick. Shit, the drinks are on Will!" The two Caucasian females go up to the table, pull out their seats and sit at the table. The waitress comes back, and the players order some more drinks. The two females laugh, joke and flirt with the players. The clubbies just enjoy their beers and the show with the players and the females.

CHAPTER THIRTEEN

Outside the clubhouse, there is a long table with food set up. Fitzy is arranging some things on the table. The clubbies all line up to get some food. Tony is also helping out. Fitzy said, "Okay gentlemen go ahead and help yourselves. I hope you guys enjoy it but try not to makes such a mess. You all have earned this, so lunch is on me." The Players start filing in and they head straight for the tables. "Hello guys, feel free to dig in. There is plenty, but if need be I'll go get some more," Fitzy Said.

Dan said, "All right Fitzy good job man. We certainly appreciate it, but we wish you were on the home side." Fitzy was known to treat the players and clubbies with some pretty good food from time to time. He used money from his own pocket. "No problem. Is there anything you guys need or want to discuss with me, Tony or the clubbies?" Fitzy asked. "No, we just feel they are doing an excellent job here and all their hard work is really starting to pay off," Dan said as he took a bite out of a hotdog.

Fitzy, with a big smile on his face, said "You guys heard that? I told you everything is going to be fine. You see what can be done with a little teamwork? The players really appreciate it." The players all stop eating and loading their plates momentarily to give the clubbies a round of applause. They form sort of a line, and they all shake each clubbies' hand. Later, in the home-side clubhouse, Fitzy is looking through boxes full of equipment. The boxes contain gloves, Jerseys, shoes and caps. The equipment belonged to the players but is set to be discarded. The word discard is written across each box in black magic marker. Tony is also there.

"They're going to throw all this stuff away Tony?" Fitzy asked. Tony looked at Fitzy as if he was asking him a stupid question. "Yeah, that's what I was told. Every single box is supposed to be discarded," Tony replied. Fitzy picks up some of the clothing items as well as the other items and holds them up to look at them. Fitzy said, "This shit is still in good condition." Tony knew what Fitzy was going to do with the items. "Yeah I know, but I was told to discard it." Fitzy took one more look at the items, then at Tony. "Well, just let me take this stuff off your hands. I mean if it's going to be discarded anyway," Fitzy said.

PREDATOR ON THE DIAMOND: THE BOSTON RED SOX YOUTH MOLESTATION STORY

Tony, shaking his head asked, "what did you have in mind to do with it?" Fitzy fumbles through several more boxes. He holds up a pair of sneakers that appear to be in pretty good shape. "Look at this! This stuff is all in decent shape so why throw it away? We can get the players to autograph this stuff, and then I can hand it out to the clubbies." Tony was somewhat hesitant. Tony never actually saw Fitzy doing anything unusual with the clubbies. However, he was beginning to wonder if his affection for these young boys was innocent. He was starting to put things together since word got back to him about Fitzy touching the boys.

"I don't see it being a problem Fitzy. Go ahead and take that stuff out of here. Hey, I was just doing what I was told," Tony said. Fitzy thanked Tony with a big smile. He knew this would help him win the clubbies over. Inside the clubhouse, the next day, Fitzy has the boxes of supplies and equipment sitting on the floor. The clubbies are also present, and Fitzy gets some of the equipment and starts handing it out to the clubbies. With his usual smile, Fitzy said, "I told you guys that if you take care of these players for me, I will take care of you. So, here is some stuff I got for you guys. I had some of the players put their autographs on some of the equipment."

The clubbies lined up to get their equipment. They are all very happy and they start trying on some of the clothing articles and equipment. Some even swap articles of clothing. It is clear he has made them very happy and therefore he appears to be happy too. It makes him feel good to see them happy.

CHAPTER FOURTEEN

Will decided to visit his father. His father's name is Roy and he lived just blocks away. This was somewhat unusual, but it actually worked out pretty good. Will did at least know where his father lived and knew who his father was. However, his father's relationship with him and the family was not that close ironically. Roy was sitting in his reclining lounge chair watching television. Will was standing near the front door, looking down and fumbling with his hands. "So, you okay Will?" Roy asked.

Will told Roy that he and everyone was fine. Roy gets up and moves some stuff off the couch. "Have a seat and make yourself at home," Roy said as he practically fell back into his chair. Will looked around the untidy house for a second and said, "No thanks, I need to get going. I have to get back to the ballpark." "Can I get you something?" Roy asked. Will told Roy he was okay. Roy takes some money out of his pocket and approaches Will. "Here you go Will, take this," Roy said as he held out the money in his hand. Will just stood there for a second.

It was like he was reluctant to take his father's money. It was certainly not the first time. In fact, that was the main reason him and his brother stopped by there from time to time. He just did not want it to be so obvious. On some occasions, Will and his brother would go over and touch up Roy's yard. He felt he was earning his father's money that way. "That's okay," Will said with a sense of confidence. Roy took Will's hand and put the money in it. After all, it was Roy's way of showing he still cared. However, Will and his brother needed more.

They needed Roy to be there for them. "Just take it Will. You guys do a great job on my yard, and I appreciate that. By the way, are you guys going to come by tomorrow and touch it up?" Will put the money in his pocket rather quickly and said, "Yeah, we can do that tomorrow. Me and Larry will come take care of it tomorrow morning." Roy thanked him and asked, "How are you doing in school?" "I am doing okay," Will responded. Roy, with a half-smile, said "Well that's good, I'm glad to hear that. I'm sorry I haven't made it to your games, but I'm sure you understand." Will did not understand, and it crushed him not to see his father in the stands. Will turns to exit, but looks over his shoulder and says, "Yeah I understand... Okay, I need to get back over to the ball-park."

PREDATOR ON THE DIAMOND: THE BOSTON RED SOX YOUTH MOLESTATION STORY

Roy walks Will to the door. He can clearly see something is not right with Will. Will was always generally quiet, but he seemed very distant, like he was not himself. The things he was experiencing at the ballpark were definitely heavy on his mind. "Will are you sure you're okay? I mean you don't seem to be yourself," Roy said. "Yeah I'm fine," Will advised as he left the house shaking his head.

Later on, at the ballpark clubhouse visitor's locker room, a Caucasian ball player, Phil, sits on the bench near his locker. He looks around to make sure the coast is clear. Dave, the clubby, approaches him. Dave is also looking around. Dave takes out a bag of cocaine and gives it to Phil. Phil holds the bag up to check it out. He then opens the bag to put some on the tip of his tongue. "Thanks Dave you got a real good one this time. It looks like these boys in Winter Haven are taking care of us," Phil said with a smile.

Phil puts the cocaine in his locker and closes the locker. He continued saying, "Yeah that was definitely a good one. Either they're taking care of us or they're getting better stuff," Dave continued to look around to make sure nobody saw him make this exchange. He said, "they said they would take care of you guys because they're your fans. They said you guys take good care of them, so they are going to return the favor. In fact, he wanted me to let you guys know that."

Dave pulled out a fresh one-hundred-dollar bill from the drug purchase and attempts to return it to Phil. "Oh, I almost forgot to give you this," Dave said with the bill in his outstretched hand. Phil slowly and easily pushes Dave's hand away and says, "You don't owe me anything man! You keep that shit." Dave stuffs the money back in his pocket rather quickly as if he's expecting Phil to change his mind. "Thanks!" Dave shouted. Phil put his finger over his own mouth to give Dave the hush symbol. "Shhhh!" Phil said.

Phil opens his locker back up. He hands Dave some more cash. It's another crisp hundred-dollar bill. "In fact, here's a little something for your time and trouble," Phil said. Dave's mouth dropped open with surprise and excitement. "Wow! Thanks!" Dave said. Dave stuffs the money in his pockets, which are now bulging with cash. Phil takes the bag of cocaine out of his locker once again. Holding it up he asked Dave, "You want some of this shit?" Dave, with a few seconds of thought said, "Not now, but maybe another time." "Okay my man, you know I got you," Phil responded as he put the drugs back into his locker and slapped Dave five.

CHAPTER FIFTEEN

Will was walking down the hallway of the high school with his best friend Tim. The Principal, Mr. Roberts, who is a Caucasian man, comes down the hallway. He stops in front of Will and puts his hands on his hips. "Will, I need you to go to my office right now!" Mr. Roberts said with a rather serious face. Will looked to be somewhat intimidated. "What's the matter Mr. Roberts?" Will queried. Mr. Roberts appeared to be getting upset as he turned red. "Just go there and wait for me, I need to talk to you! Better yet, you just come with me to the office right now," Mr. Roberts said.

Mr. Roberts escorted Will to his office and pointed to a chair for Will to have a seat. Will sat down and looked around at some of the pictures the principal had in his office. Mr. Roberts sat at his desk and said, "I just wanted to tell you that I don't appreciate what you're doing around here boy." Will, with a confused look, replied "What are you talking about Mr. Roberts?" "You know what I am talking about! You need to hang with the colored folks and stay away from the white folks," Mr. Roberts said quite seriously as he looked right into Will's eyes.

Will's mouth hangs open as he is rather shocked. He never knew the principal felt this way about him. Certainly, many of his classmates and friends did not have the same sentiment. "Now this is the only warning you're going to get. If you keep on hanging with the white students, I will make sure you don't graduate from here. Is that clear?" Mr. Roberts continued. Will, still shocked, said "Yes Mr. Roberts." "Good, now go!" Mr. Roberts barked out to Will causing him to jump. Will leaves still looking puzzled. Tim walks up to him as he leaves and confronts him. He could tell by the expression on Will's face that the meeting did not go well. "What's up Will? Are you in trouble?" Tim asked.

"Yeah you can say that. Mr. Roberts doesn't want me hanging around with you because you're white and I'm black. He doesn't want me to hang with whites. He said I should hang with my own kind," Will said with disappointment. Tim said, "Seriously? He told you that?" Will let Tim know he was not kidding. He also told him he did not know what he could do about it because a lot of his friends were white. "He can't tell you that man! He can't tell you who to be friends with." Will, with a low chuckle, said "Yeah, well why don't you go in there and tell him that."

Tim, now confused, stopped dead in his tracks. He then asked, "You're still my friend right?" Will replied, "Of course I'm still your friend and we can hang out, but not here at the school man." Tim, with a sigh of relief, said "Hey dude I just wanted to make sure." Mr. Roberts was okay with Will when he was helping the school's basketball team win, but he felt Will was out of his place when he hung with these guys. As the two of them walked out of the school building, Mr. Roberts watched them from his window, which had the blinds open. He crossed his arms and shook his head. Will looked over and saw Mr. Roberts.

Will paused for a second and looked surprised. "Well, I am going to grab something from the cafeteria and then I'm going out to the ballpark," Will said. "Okay man I'll see you later and don't worry about that asshole," Tim said as Will walked back into the school. The next day Fitzy stands outside the visitor's side dugout. It is pre-game and the players practice. He stands at a distance, sort of in the shadows. He is watching the young kids catch foul balls in an open area near the stands. Fitzy pays particular attention to two young black boys that were there catching and chasing foul balls. Fitzy drove the cart over to where they were. He managed to give them a ride on the cart.

Fitzy used this approach to recruit and/or molest more young boys. He would even give them a tour of the clubhouse and locker areas. It was not unusual for him to spend countless hours during spring training games watching young boys. His clubbies were well trained and did not need to be micro-managed. This freed him up for these types of activities. After the game was over, Will was sweeping the clubhouse area right outside the umpires' room. One of the other young black clubbies comes out of the umpires' room which was previously closed.

Will stands there watching as the young clubby zips and buckles his pants. The young black clubby is visibly upset and walks away rather quickly. Fitzy comes from the Umpire's room, looks at Will, smiles and starts rubbing his hands together as if he has found another prey. "Hey buddy. How's it going? Long time no see," Fitzy said as Will slowly backs up and then turns around to leave. "Come on buddy, where you going so fast?" Fitzy asked. Will walked to the laundry room area of the clubhouse where there are several other clubbies working. He is very nervous and looks around like he's being chased by the mob. Fitzy comes in, but then leaves rather quickly after he sees the other clubbies.

CHAPTER SIXTEEN

Troy, Michael, Tim, and Brad are over at Will's house. There are three white females also there. Their names are, Darlene, Sissy and Janice. Shirley fixes them all a wonderful meal. She sets the food on the table as Will and all his friends grab a seat. There are just enough seats to accommodate everyone. Shirley enjoyed playing hostess to Will and his friends. She realized how much Will loved being with his friends. His friends were very respectable around Shirley and addressed her as ma'am when they spoke to her.

"Let me see if I can get you guys' names right. Troy, Michael, Tom, Brad, Darlene, Sissy and Janice," Shirley said with a smile. She just knew she had it right this time. Every time they came over, it was a challenge to name everyone correctly. Will and his friends all laughed. Will shook his head no and said, "Mom you got all the names right except for Tim. You called him Tom." Shirley excused herself and apologized to Tim. "Okay well, excuse me Tim," she said.

Shirley looked around for a second and then asked, "Will where's Larry?" Will said, "I think he's still out at the ballpark." Larry generally spent more time at the ballpark than Will. The two of them seldom interacted at the ballpark. They did not really even communicate much. They both were experiencing some of the same things at the ballpark with Fitzy. There was sort of a shame and embarrassment factor that seemed to come between them. "Well, I guess that should be enough for everyone," Shirley said as she got ready to go to work. "Yeah mom this should be okay," Will acknowledged.

Shirley, wiping off the cabinets said, "Okay, Will I have to get back over to the flower shop. You guys try not to mess up my kitchen." "Don't worry momma, I'll make sure everything is taken care of," Will assured her. They all thanked Shirley, waved goodbye to her and proceed to dig in. The next day, Will was in the clubhouse visitor's side area with several other clubbies. They are all cleaning up and getting equipment ready after a game. One of the black players from the visiting team, Nate, signals Will. "Hey Will come here for a minute," he says to Will who is still nervous and confused.

PREDATOR ON THE DIAMOND: THE BOSTON RED SOX YOUTH MOLESTATION STORY

Will walked over to Nate rather slowly and with a little reluctance. "What's up?" Will replied. "Come on and walk with me to my locker," Nate requested. Will seemed to be a little more nervous at this point. It was unusual for any player to take a walk and talk with Will in this manner. Will's anxiety came from the unknown. The only other adult to talk to him that way and isolate him from the rest of the players and clubbies was Fitzy. He wondered what this player could possibly want with him. "Why, what's up? Will made a final inquiry. Nate just looked at Will with a sarcastic look and shaking his head said, "Come on man, just talk with me. I need to chat with you for a second."

Will strolled to Nate's locker with Nate. Will leans on the lockers and once again asked, "Okay what's up?" Nate looked around to make sure the coast was clear, disregarding his teammates who were there. "I needed to ask you something, but first I need to let you know this has to stay between me and you." Will, still curious, said "Yeah, okay go ahead." "Would you go over to "The Spot" and get me some stuff?" Will, with a puzzled look, said "Some stuff?" "Yeah, you know, some coke man. You know any cats over there that sell the good shit?" Will was surprised at the question. His first thought was to play stupid.

However, after a few seconds of thought, Will said, "Umm yeah, I know a few cats over there that do that. They are not really my friends, but I see them," Will said as he looked around. "Well, can you do me a huge favor?" Nate asked as he too looked around. "Sure, what do you need?" Will inquired. "If I give you the cash would you go down to "The Spot" and get me some good stuff?" Nate asked, almost begging. Will agreed to do what Nate requested after pretending he did not know what Nate wanted. Nate pulls some cash from his pocket and hands it to Will. Will looks surprised.

"Here's a hundred-dollar bill and here's a fifty, so there you have one hundred fifty dollars. Just get me what you can with that. I'll take care of you when you bring it to me. Let them know it's for a baseball player and they should take care of you. Those boys up in Chelsea, Massachusetts treat us right." "Okay I'm cool with that," Will agreed with a look of surprise on his face. It was as if he knew he would be getting paid nicely for doing this service for Nate. Nate thanked Will and said, "That's cool Will! I knew you would take care of me. Now, you know you have to keep this quiet right?" "Yeah, I won't tell anyone," Will said as he continued to look around.

He then took the money and quickly put it in his pocket. "Good, that's my man! So how is your brother doing?" Nate asked as if he had genuine concern. Will said, "He's okay; he still works on the other side, so I don't get to see him or talk to him too much here at the park." "Yeah, he used to take care of us sometimes when he worked on this side," Nate remarked. Will was pretty surprised by that statement. It was the first time anyone had made mention of that to him.

Oh, he had heard stories and rumors about what was going on around the clubhouse and even seen a lot. However, he often chose not to get involved. "Yeah, he was our main man," Nate said with a smile on his face. He wanted Will to become another clubby who helped him out in the inner-city neighborhoods. "Okay I will take care of it. I'll have the stuff for you by next game, is that good?" Will asked. "Yeah that's perfect. We can meet right here." Will turned and walked away. Nate just shook his head and smiled as Will walked away.

CHAPTER SEVENTEEN

In Winter Haven, Will cruises on his bike through a rough neighborhood. He pulls up to a place called, "The Spot." Will is greeted by a couple of drug dealers. Big Jay and Little Tee approach Will's bike. Will appears to be extremely nervous. After all, this was his first time actually buying drugs. He had seen them being sold in the neighborhoods, but never really got involved in that activity. He had tried pot before with one of his friends, but he preferred drinking more.

Big Jay, looking around, asked, "Hey man, what can we do for you?" Will takes out the cash and replied, "Here you go. This is from one of the baseball players. He told me to tell you to fix them up with the usual." Big Jay counts the money as Little Tee stands in front of the bike. Big Jay yelled, "Okay man you heard him! Take care of him." Little Tee pulls out a bag of coke and holds it up for Will to see.

Will, with a puzzled look, said, "I guess that one is cool." Big Jay snatched the bag, and yelled, "Hell no man! We can't do them players like that. Take care of them damn players!" Little Tee pulled out another bag rather quickly and said, "Now this one right here is cool for sure man." Little Tee just shook his head, because he knew he was wrong for trying to cheat Will. Big Jay wanted to stay in business with the baseball players. Big Jay took the bag from Will and held it up. "Yeah that one looks cool. Tell them players we got their connection right here," Big Jay said, pumping his fist.

Will took the bag and assured Big Jay he would pass on the word. "That's cool little brother. So, what's your name? I am just asking, because I need to let these cats know who's coming through here," Big Jay inquired. Will was reluctant to say his name to these two drug dealers. He did not know them and therefore he became nervous when they asked him his name. "Oh, they call me Will," he finally responded. Big Jay slaps Will five and says, "Okay, Will, if you guys need anything from me just let me know." Will seemed to be a little more relaxed. The transaction was nearly complete, and it didn't seem to be as bad as he thought it would be. It was looking like he would get out of there alive. "What's your name man?" Will boldly asked.

"All you need to know is that I'm the number one man around here and they call me Big Jay for short." Will rides away rather quickly. Big Jay slaps his partners five and sort of does some dance moves. "That's what I'm talking about man! We about to be big time! You know why? We got the baseball player connection going on now and all Spring," Big Jay bragged. Big Jay pulled out the cash and started counting it as Will disappeared into the night. The next day, the high school principal, Mr. Roberts, goes into an office that belongs to Coach Sanders. Coach Sanders is fixing up and arranging things on his desk.

His office trophy display case has several conference championship trophies. His desk has pictures of his family, while the wall is reserved for portraits with him and the school basketball team. As he turned around, he is startled by Mr. Roberts' sudden appearance. "I wanted to talk to you, is this a bad time?" Mr. Roberts asked with a stone face. Coach Sanders looked at the clock on the wall and said, "Well, I was just about to head out of here for basketball practice." Coach Sanders was somewhat surprised and curious. Mr. Roberts seldom visited the coach unless there was something on his mind to discuss.

PREDATOR ON THE DIAMOND: THE BOSTON RED SOX YOUTH MOLESTATION STORY

"I know how you like to be on time for basketball practice. This shouldn't take too long," Mr. Roberts said, as he helped himself to a seat. "Okay, I'm all ears," Coach Sanders acknowledged. Mr. Roberts advised the coach he wanted to talk to him about Will. Coach Sanders could tell by Mr. Roberts' expression it was not something good. "What about Will? Is he in some sort of trouble?" Mr. Roberts crossed his arms and just looked at the coach for a second. "Well, basically I want you to bench him until further notice," Mr. Roberts said. The coach rolled his desk chair out and took a seat. It was as if he needed to take a load off.

Mr. Roberts did not seem to make sense. Will was one of their best players. "Bench Will? Why?" The coach asked. "Yeah, I want him benched! He disrespected me. He wants to try me, but obviously he is forgetting who's in charge around here. I can make his stay here very unpleasant," Mr. Roberts blurted out. Coach Sanders shook his head in disbelief. "You do realize Will is the best and most productive player on the team right?" He reminded Mr. Roberts. Mr. Roberts replied, "Yes I am well aware of Will's performance on the court, but I don't care. I don't want him playing!" The coach could not fathom having Will benched.

"Are you sure you want me to do that? I mean, is there some other punishment we can give him? Coach Sanders inquired. Mr. Roberts jumped up suddenly. He began to pace the floor with his hands clasped behind him. He just looked at the coach with resentment. "No, there isn't!" Mr. Roberts said. He starts to storm away but stops and turns around once again. "I want the son of a bitch benched and I mean that!" Mr. Roberts said as he left Coach Sander's room and slammed the door. Coach Sanders just shakes his head and slams his fist on his desk. He never got a chance to know exactly what Will did to piss him off, but he would surely talk to Will to find out.

CHAPTER EIGHTEEN

About a week later, Winter Haven basketball team had a home game. The scoreboard read, "Home 60 Visitor 62." Four seconds remain. Coach Sanders has taken a time out and the cheerleaders do a routine on the floor. The crowd chants, "Will! Will! Will!" However, Will is not playing. He has been benched as requested by the principal. Will is clearly upset, as he just sits there with a long face and with his arms crossed. This was the first time Will was not in the line-up. The players, including James, a Caucasian player, are all gathered around Coach Sanders who is in the middle of the circle.

Will just stays on the bench looking sad. Coach Sanders looks over to him and shrugs his shoulders. He had already told Will his benching was the principal's decision, and he had no say in the matter. Coach Sanders takes a few seconds to look around the circle of players. Suddenly, Will does appear in the circle. "James needs to take that shot," Will said confidently. Coach Sanders took one more look around the circle and then over to his bench. "James, you are going to have to take that shot," The coach said in agreement with Will. James had never taken the role of the "go to" guy in any game. The ball would have almost always gone to Will. "You want me to take the shot Coach Sanders? Man, we need Will in here. I don't know if I can make it," James said.

Coach Sanders did another quick look at his bench. He just shook his head and said, "Look, I can't play him, and I don't have anyone else who I trust to take the shot. So, we are going to have to improvise. Now we can do this, so let's have a little confidence guys." Coach Sanders takes out his mini white board and marker to illustrate what he wants. "I need you, you and you to be ready to crash the boards for the rebound. You are going to inbound the ball directly to James. James, you just need to be ready and remember we only have four seconds. We don't necessarily need a three-pointer, so let's just take what they give us," The coach instructed the team.

The buzzer signifying the end of the time out rings. "Okay, here we go on three. One, two, three!" The Coach yells. The players all shout, "Winter Haven!" They hit the floor going full speed. A player inbounds the ball to James. James gets by two defenders and takes the shot with one second left. He misses the shot, and the once noisy crowd is now silent. The players just drop their heads and head to the lockers as the visiting team celebrates on the court. Coach Sanders looks at Will, shakes his head and follows the team to the lockers. Will just sits there holding his head down, even after his team has cleared the floor. Not being able to contribute to his team, as well as what he was experiencing at the ballpark, was definitely having a profound effect on him.

PREDATOR ON THE DIAMOND: THE BOSTON RED SOX YOUTH MOLESTATION STORY

The next day, Coach Sanders was sitting in his office finishing up some paperwork. There is a knock on his door. Coach Sanders yells, "It's open!" Will pushes the door open and walks in. "Will, what can I do for you young man? I would be willing to bet it has something to do with you being benched, but I thought I made everything clear to you," the coach tells Will. Will knew it was the principal who was responsible for him being benched, but he also knew he would not be able to change his mind. The coach would be his best shot at getting back in the starting line-up. "Coach Sanders, I just want to know how much longer," Will asked curiously.

Coach Sanders paused and looked up to the ceiling for a short period. "Unfortunately, I can't answer that. Mr. Roberts said it would be until further notice. I assume the further notice will come from him." "But this ain't even fair! I haven't done anything wrong," Will proclaimed. Coach Sanders dropped his head into his hands and said, "Hey, I believe you Will, but my hands are tied." Tears began to well up in Will's eyes. "I'm getting punished for no reason," Will said, as a tear rolled down his cheek. "Can you talk to him again?" Will asked as he wiped the tear away. "I will, but I don't think it's going to do any good. I think his mind is already made up," Coach Sanders said. Will dropped his head and the tears started to flow more freely. He was clearly crushed.

The coach just shook his head. He was feeling sympathetic towards Will, but he felt there was nothing he could do. "Well then I might as well quit the team!" Will shouted defiantly. Coach Sanders had to just think about that remark for a second. He had to think of something to say to change Will's mind. He tried a little reversed psychiatry and said, "You don't have to do that Will. If you do that you let him win. Just hang in there and we'll get you back in there." "Sitting on the bench is killing me, I hate it!" Will replied. Coach Sanders walked over to Will and put his hand on Will's shoulder to sort of comfort him. Will jumped a bit and just looked at the coach.

He had never reacted towards the coach like that, but once again, the actions of Fitzy were affecting him. "I can understand how you feel, and believe me, watching you sitting there is killing all of us. However, you do need to hang in there like I said," Coach Sanders said. Will reluctantly agreed with the coach and said, "Okay, I guess I will wait a while longer." A smile came over the coach. After all he knew Will was not a quitter. "That's what I want to hear. There are no quitters on my team." The coach assured Will. Will walked out with a renewed sense of pride. He would not let the principal win.

CHAPTER NINETEEN

At the Chain of Lakes ballpark, Will was standing around chatting with a few of the baseball players before practice. Fitzy comes up behind Will and begins rubbing and massaging his shoulders. Will is startled and jumps, whipping his head around to see who was doing this to him. "Hey Will, how's it going buddy?" Fitzy asked. Will just slips from under Fitzy's grasp, turns around and gives Fitzy a mean look and walks away.

Fitzy looked at the other players and clubbies with a look of surprise and discontentment. Fitzy did not like to be rejected by the young clubbies, especially publicly. "What the hell is his problem?" Fitzy asked as he threw his arms up. One of the Caucasian players said, "I don't know Fitzy, maybe he doesn't like you. Maybe he's not your type." The players all started laughing and walked away. Fitzy did not find it to be amusing. He wanted the players and clubbies to look up to him as a kind and caring person not as the monster he really was. The next day, a Caucasian player from the visiting team, Dennis, was waiting in the clubhouse equipment room. Will goes in the room and closes the door. The player hands him some cash. Will stuffs the cash in his pocket rather quickly without even counting it.

Will really was wondering where the other player, Nate, was at. He was really not too comfortable with the change. "I am giving you extra cash this time. Now you can get some for yourself and your buddies if you want," Dennis said. Will nodded his head with acknowledgement. "I want some coke and some pot. Just get me whatever you can buy with that," Dennis said, as he was trying to make things clear.

Will said he understood. "Will, you know you're the man now right? Word is out that you know how to get good shit," Dennis said with a sense of urgency. This was something he wanted Will to grasp. He wanted Will to feel like doing this for the players was putting him in an important position. Dennis stuck out his hand and Will slapped him five. "Yeah I know," Will said with a sense of pride and satisfaction. "We're going to take care of you if you just take care of us," Dennis told Will. "Don't worry, I will take care of you guys," Will assured Dennis.

Will liked the players and liked being their man. He felt accepted and respected by the players. Later that afternoon, Will was driving one of the baseball player's cars through Winter Haven. He sees Fitzy's vehicle parked on one of the neighborhood streets. As he proceeds to slow down, he sees Fitzy walking up the block with a box of goodies in his arms. A small mob of young black boys, and even some young girls, swarm Fitzy practically knocking him down.

PREDATOR ON THE DIAMOND: THE BOSTON RED SOX YOUTH MOLESTATION STORY

Fitzy hands out the goodies from the box. Will pulls over, parks the car and turns down the car stereo. He watches Fitzy for a while. Suddenly, Will flies into a rage and begins pounding on the steering wheel. "No! No! No!" He shouted. He then punches the gas and takes off. The next evening, Shirley was sitting on the couch with her head leaning back. She had on her work clothes, but she was very ill. Will, Larry, Lisa and Lynn were also in the living room standing over Shirley. "Momma are you going to be okay?" Will asked, as he sat on the couch next to Shirley.

Shirley, with a soft, weak voice said, "Momma is not feeling too well, but I am still going to work this evening." They all looked at each other, surprised and worried. Even though the boys of the family did what they could to help out, their mother was still the one who supported them. She seldom took time off work. "Momma you can't go to work like this," Will said, almost begging. Shirley completely stretched out on the couch and said, "Just give me a few minutes to rest and I will be fine. Wake me up in about half an hour." Larry tucked one of the couch pillows under Shirley's head, as he looked at the others and shook his head. He was signifying to them she was not to be awakened. Things would get tough around there if Shirley was unable to work. Will and his brother Larry were not making enough money at the ballpark to support the family.

His older brother Jim had practically moved out and mostly lived with his girlfriend. Lisa was still in elementary school and Lynn was only able to help out a little around the house. Will really loved his mother and felt he may have to step up his game at the ballpark. He loved his mother and would do anything for her. Even if he had to do things he knew were wrong with Fitzy. He knew he and his brother would both need to step it up to help Shirley out. Shirley did not make it to work and unfortunately, she had to be rushed to the hospital that evening.

CHAPTER TWENTY

Will stopped by his father's house, because he really wanted to talk to him about some of the things that were happening to him. Most of the time, Will bottled his feelings up inside, because he did not believe his father cared about him. Oh, sure his father would give him money once in a while, but they really lost their connection when him and his mother separated. Sadly, he grew up watching his father abuse his mother. He still loved him though. He just would rather talk to his mother or older brothers when he had a problem.

Sometimes he would even confide in his male friends from the high school or the clubbies from the ballpark. Now that his mother was in the hospital, the men of the house would definitely need to be strong. As Roy let Will in his house, Will could see just how bad things had gotten for Roy. Roy staggered into the living room and flopped on the couch after letting Will in. Several empty wine bottles littered the coffee table and dining room table. The place looked like a teen party was held there with trash everywhere. "What's up son? What are you up to?" Roy said, as he leaned his head back. Will stayed standing, because as usual, there really was no place clean to sit.

Will's first thought was to just turn around and leave. He felt perhaps he could catch him when he was sober. "Daddy, momma is not feeling too well. She went to the hospital," Will said as he began to get misty-eyed. Roy just sat there quietly for a moment. When what Will said finally did sink in, Roy managed to open his eyes and sit up. "What's wrong with her?" Roy asked. "I don't know," Will said looking down sadly. "What the hell do you want me to do about it?" Roy said as he took his wallet out. He then opened his wallet and turned it upside down. Shaking it he said, "I don't have no Goddamn money, so what do y'all want from me?" Will turned around to leave.

He knew he was not getting anywhere with his father in this condition. He began to realize his going there was a mistake. He wished he was able to connect with his father. He wanted to talk to his father about some of the things that were happening at the ballpark. He wanted to be able to talk to his father about many things. Will stormed out of Roy's house in tears. The next week, Will was in the clubhouse visitor's locker room before a practice. Will saw a Hispanic baseball player, Jose, taking a drug he had not seen before. Will confronted Jose, and Jose told him it was something to make him stronger and faster. Will did not know these drugs were known as steroids.

A little later, Will met with Dennis. Will told Dennis that he could not get drugs as much anymore. Dennis agreed but had a rather harsh and scary threat he made to Will. He told Will there would be severe consequences if he went to anyone about the drug sales or drug use. Will had no idea why the player would threaten him. He just knew he would not be able to make the extra cash he was making at the ballpark. Money he desperately needed and wanted. Will was starting to believe, everything was falling apart in his life, at home, in school and at the ballpark. He felt there was no way out and few people to turn to. Will walked away, looked around to make sure the coast was clear, and went into his little duffel bag.

He pulled out a bottle of wine and took a big gulp. At this point, beer was not helping him get through his pain, even though beer was much more accessible. There were times when he would smoke marijuana and drink at the same time. He had even tried coke. Later, Will went into the equipment room to gather his thoughts. It was a place he sometimes went to hide. He saw Fitzy holding down one of the younger clubbies. Fitzy is trying to undo the clubby's pants with one hand and holding him down with the other. "It's going to be all right little buddy just relax," Fitzy said still struggling with the young boy. Fitzy looked up and saw Will just standing there.

While Fitzy is distracted, the young clubby gets away from him and runs out of the equipment room. "How's it going buddy?" Will turns around to leave. Fitzy asked, "Where you going little buddy?" As he caught up to Will and grabbed him by his shoulder. For some reason, on this day, Will did not have the fight in him. Psychologically he wanted to lash out at Fitzy. Will whipped around, almost confrontationally to see what Fitzy wanted. "Just take it easy my young buddy," Fitzy said as he worked his way behind Will and began to massage his shoulders. Will tensed up at first, but then relaxed. "Whoa little buddy, you're a little tense!" Fitzy said as he continued to massage Will's shoulders.

"Look buddy... I heard about what you have been going through. Nothing that happens to any of you guys gets passed me. But just like I told you from day one, I can take care of you. Nobody is going to take care of you like me," Fitzy reminded Will. Fitzy was saying things that Will needed to hear at that point in time, and the shoulder massage was relaxing. "Here is what I can do for you... I can talk to your principal. Then, I can put in a word for you with the staff and players around here. Before you know it you will be the top clubby around here. You will be a star at your school again too."

PREDATOR ON THE DIAMOND: THE BOSTON RED SOX YOUTH MOLESTATION STORY

"You can really do that for me?" Will inquired. Fitzy turned Will around to make sure he had his undivided attention. With one of his hands still on Will's shoulders, he said, "I have been telling you all along what I can do for you, but you haven't been listening. In fact, you told our little secret and almost got me in trouble," Fitzy advised. Will was confused and frustrated. He knew Fitzy's kind gestures would come at a price. A price he felt he would not want to pay. He knew exactly what Fitzy would want from him. However, he felt there was a way for him to get around it. After all, he had managed to avoid Fitzy's advances up to this point. Fitzy reached in his back pocket and pulled out his wallet. He gave Will two crisp one-hundred-dollar bills.

Will just stood there. "Take that for you and your family," Fitzy said. "Now get out there and get to work!" Fitzy continued. As Will turned around to leave, Fitzy smacked him on his buttocks. Will turned around briefly to take a glance at Fitzy. Fitzy winked at Will and smiled. Will just continued towards the exit. "Remember, if you want to be the number one clubby around here, you will have to learn to keep your mouth shut. Now, I have already done damage control from what you said about me to some of the players. In order for us to work together you are going to have to apologize, and say it was all a misunderstanding," Fitzy said.

Will just stood there looking at Fitzy as if he were crazy. Will did not want to apologize for something he was not wrong about. However, he did agree to apologize. Will would do anything to get things back to the way they were. He still loved being around the professional baseball players and working at the ballpark, in general.

CHAPTER TWENTY-ONE

Will tries to creep into the house. It is late night or what you could call early morning. Will is clearly drunk and high, as he sort of stumbles his way into the house. Jimmy has returned home to help out and has assumed a stronger role as man of the house. Shirley is still sick. She is out of the hospital and limited to bed rest at home. Jimmy is upset with Will, because of his recent behavior and he lets him know about it. "So, I see you thought you could sneak in here huh? Where have you been? Momma is up in bed sick and you're out there running the Goddamn streets! Don't you know we need you to help us out around here?" "Look man, I was just hanging out with some of the players," Will said with slurred speech. Jimmy knew Will was lying. Larry had been home a long time from the ballpark and had already helped around the house. "Come on now, Will, you know you're not supposed to be hanging with all those adults. Mom keeps telling you that. By the way, I saw you get out of Fitzy's car."

"Boy, you're not supposed to be coming in the house this late on a school night. Just look at you man! You can hardly stand up. You better hope mom doesn't see you like this," Jimmy said as he grabbed Will by his shoulders to hold him up. "Man, I was just having a good time. Why are you sweating me?" Will asked as he leaned against the wall to support himself. Jimmy let Will go as Will continued to lean against the wall. "You are running the streets like you're crazy when you really need to be studying them books. You think you're going to be some basketball star or something? Boy, you need to hit them books like I said," Jimmy advised Will. "Okay, I'll do better dad, now can I go to bed?" Will said sarcastically.

Jimmy knew Will was letting the alcohol talk for him. If he were sober he would not have this sarcastic tone. Jimmy felt it was still important for him to let Will know who the older brother is and who is in charge. "No! You go to bed when I tell you to. Now I'm not going to take your bullshit!" Jimmy said as he grabbed Will by his shirt and pulled him close to him. Will pulled away and said, "Get off me!" Will then started to walk away. "Yeah, you better get your ass upstairs and go to bed before I knock you out," Jimmy said as he allowed Will to walk upstairs.

PREDATOR ON THE DIAMOND: THE BOSTON RED SOX YOUTH MOLESTATION STORY

It was plain to see things around there were going from bad to worse. Jimmy knew what Will was going through, because he too was sexually abused by Fitzy years prior as a clubby. He believed Larry was also dealing with sexual abuse by Fitzy. None of the boys dared to speak to each other about their encounters with Fitzy. Many of the clubbies did not even discuss their encounters with Fitzy with each other.

Jeff, a ten-year-old black clubby, walked into the clubhouse laundry room at the Chain of Lakes Training facility. Fitzy sneaks in behind him and stands watching him work for a few seconds. He then closes the door and locks it. Jeff is startled and looks frightened. "How are you doing there Jeff? Long time no see," Fitzy said. Jeff replied, "I'm doing fine, Mr. Fitzpatrick." Fitzy had that intimidating smirk on his face.

Fitzy positioned himself in front of the door to prevent the young clubby from leaving. "You ready to play that little game we play? You know, our secret game," Fitzy asked. Jeff stood there looking scared. He did not want to play any games with Fitzy. "No, I need to go home. My mom wants me there," Jeff warned. Fitzy crossed his arms with discontentment. Even though Fitzy was molesting several of the clubbies, he had the ones he came back to often.

It was not unusual for him to attempt to molest several clubbies in the same day. There were times when he was unable to get some of them alone. "Oh, come on Jeff, what the hell is your problem boy? I just want to help you out. I help you guys out, but you guys don't want to help me out," Fitzy said. When Jeff told Fitzy he just wanted to go home, Fitzy became angry. Jeff became so disturbed and upset, he wet himself. Fitzy turned up his face with displeasure. He would definitely not push the issue since Jeff was now a mess.

"Well go home Jeff! Leave now! You don't need to bother finishing up here. If you guys want to start acting like this, I will start treating you accordingly. You just made a big mistake little buddy. You see, I have connections around here. I can make it, so you never work here again," Fitzy yelled as he unlocked the door and swung it open. Jeff just puts his head down and leaves crying. Fitzy slams the door angrily. "Little Bastard! I don't care if you don't come back!" Fitzy shouted. Later that afternoon there was a ballgame going on and one of the Red Sox players hits a double. There are plenty of fans in the 7000-seat capacity stadium and nearly every seat is filled. The announcer can be heard in the background calling the play-by-play. Will is sitting in the visitor side dugout. A few of the other clubbies also watch the game from the dugout.

PREDATOR ON THE DIAMOND: THE BOSTON RED SOX YOUTH MOLESTATION STORY

There are players in the dugout, but Will sits alone. Fitzy sits next to him and puts his arm around him. Will pulls away and looks at Fitzy in a weird manner. However, he does not take Fitzy's arm off of him. "What's the matter, buddy? I just came to give you some great news. Trust me, I know you will like this, and you will definitely thank me for it," Fitzy said with a grin on his face. "What?" Will asked. Fitzy pulls out a season schedule and shows it to Will. He points to a particular spot on the paper and says, "Look what team is coming here to play us several times. You know what that means right?" Will looked at the schedule again and then back to Fitzy with a confused look and replied, "No, not really."

Fitzy looked at Will strangely. He was surprised Will did not know what he was talking about. "I'll give you a hint. It's the team that is our biggest rival," Fitzy hinted. "Oh yeah that's right, New York Yankees are coming right?" Will said. "That's right buddy, how would you like to be the lead visitor side clubby responsible for them? I mean, you would basically be their go to guy," Fitzy said. Will's eyes lit up and his mouth was wide open. He is basically speechless. Fitzy, pinching Will's lips together, said "You're welcome buddy. I told you I would take care of you buddy." Fitzy puts his hand out. Will just looks at him a few seconds, but then finally slaps him five.

Fitzy knew he had made Will's Day, perhaps his whole Spring season. "I told you buddy; I can make you big here. All you have to do is listen to what I tell you. You know by now I just want to help you guys," Fitzy reminded Will. Will wondered what he would have to do. He knew it would be something and there was most likely a catch, so he didn't ask. Fitzy told him to just be ready to work a little harder for him on the visitor's side. Will gave Fitzy a weird look. He was sure there was more. Fitzy let him know to be ready for those games.

He told Will he would be able to get some autographed memorabilia from members of the team. Will agreed to do it. Fitzy also asked Will if he wanted to take a trip to Boston. He told Will, that sometimes the players need someone to drive their cars up to Boston when the regular season starts. Will said he would see if his mother would let him. He did not know Fitzy would try to make him a guess of his condo in Boston. Fitzy puts his arm around Will's shoulder once again, but this time Will does not resist. "That's what I want to hear buddy. I just want to be your friend not your enemy."

PREDATOR ON THE DIAMOND: THE BOSTON RED SOX YOUTH MOLESTATION STORY

Some of the players who are on the bench see Fitzy with his arm around Will. They begin to whisper and laugh. Fitzy, annoyed, just sucks his teeth and gives them a mean look. He then said, "Don't pay them any mind buddy. You see that's why you need to stay with me on the visitor's side. Nobody over there will bother us." Will just shrugs his shoulders, gets up, and starts picking up the loose bats and equipment in the area. Fitzy just smiles and rubs his hands together. He then winks at Will.

CHAPTER TWENTY-TWO

Inside Fitzy's hotel room, Will is sitting in the chair near the window. He looks very nervous. Fitzy sits on the bed. This was supposedly a one-on-one meeting with Fitzy. "Look, Will you're in a lot of trouble right now buddy. You were using drugs on the premises of the ballpark. I can have you thrown out of here or even arrested if I want. Now, I let you guys drink, smoke cigarettes or chew tobacco, but you have stepped way out of line," Fitzy warned. Will reminded Fitzy he was a good clubby. He did not want to lose his job.

"I can see what I can do for you, but you have to do something for me buddy. I mean, I'm bending over backwards here to keep you out of trouble and risking my own neck," Fitzy said. Fitzy eases over to Will's chair and briefly puts his hand on Will's shoulder. Will jumps and looks at Fitzy. "Look buddy, I don't have to do anything for you. Now I can be your best friend, or your worst enemy." Will just put his head down and looks to the floor with shame.

PREDATOR ON THE DIAMOND: THE BOSTON RED SOX YOUTH MOLESTATION STORY

Fitzy starts massaging Will's shoulders. "Loosen up buddy, you're too tense. You want a couple of cold ones? I got a whole six pack in there, and believe me buddy, they're ice cold," Fitzy said. Will stops resisting. Fitzy takes out his wallet, gives Will two hundred dollars and said, "Look, I have never given out that much money at one time to any clubby. I told you; I am here to take care of you. Shit here's two hundred more buddy!" Will slowly takes the money; real reluctantly. He then goes to the refrigerator and pulls out the whole six pack. He begins slamming down the beers one by one. "Careful buddy, I don't want you too drunk now."

Will sits on the bed for a little while and then fades into a deep sleep. He begins to dream about his childhood. Will did often dream about the times he once had with his father, when he was there for them. He dreamed about the Christmases, the camping and fishing, the trips, and all the fun he and his brothers had. When Will wakes up he is still in Fitzy's hotel room bed. He jumps up to the sitting position and looks around. Fitzy is sitting on a chair watching television. Fitzy smiles and says, "Hey, sleeping beauty." Will looks down and notices that his belt is undone. He quickly buckles his pants and jumps off the bed.

"Just take it easy now buddy," Fitzy advises, now more serious. Will told Fitzy he needed to go home. He did not want to have to face his brother again. His mother, although still bedridden, was alert. She knew what was going on in the house and still tried to regulate the rules of the house. Will did not want to upset her. "You can spend the night if you want. I mean you seemed to really enjoy what I was doing to you a while ago," Fitzy told Will, once again with a smile. Will knocks over a chair, running for the room door. He unlatches all the locks and leaves rather quickly. When he leaves, he runs into a baseball player, Charles, who was in the hotel lobby area.

It was not unusual for some of the players to stay at that particular hotel. "Hey Will, what are you doing here?" the player inquired. Will just stood there speechless for a few minutes. He needed a little time to think this one out. "I was just talking to Fitzy, but I need to go home man!" Will finally blurted out. "Were you in Fitzy's room?" The player asked. Fitzy comes out to the lobby to catch up to Will. Fitzy, rubbing Will's shoulders, said "How is it going?" Speaking to Charles. "I just had a long talk with this young fellow," Fitzy continued. The player just shakes his head, turns around, and walks away.

He stops momentarily and looks at Fitzy again. "Yeah Fitzy, I bet you did," the player said with sarcasm in his voice. Charles leaves, still shaking his head. He starts mumbling, but audibly. "Nasty old bastard!" Charles remarked. Later that evening, Will is upstairs in the bathtub, scrubbing like there's no tomorrow. He rocks back and forth sobbing as he sits in a tub filled with water. There is a knock on the door and it's Shirley. Will! Are you okay in there? She yelled. Will told her he was okay, as he stopped sobbing abruptly.

Shirley advised Will to hurry up. At that point, he had been in there for two hours. It was not like Will to be in the bathroom that long, and Shirley could sense something was wrong. "I'm coming out in a second," Will said loudly. Shirley banged on the door again and asked, "Is there something wrong with you boy?" Will was reluctant to speak, because he knew his mother would detect his pain in his voice.

There were times when she was able to get things out of him even when he did not want to tell her. This was something he did not want to tell anyone about, much less his mother. He felt real confused about his sexuality. He was starting to feel like he was gay. He wondered if that was possible, even though he still found girls to be attractive. Even though he was once very popular at the school, he was still a virgin to having sex with a female.

His mother taught him to be responsible and to be careful. She actually scared him half to death about girls and sex. His father had never had that talk and walk with him. "No momma, I'm okay. I just need some time to relax," Will said. Shirley just told him to hurry up and then walked away. Will's grades were dropping, and he was beginning to miss classes. His game on the courts was even weakening, which meant more time on the bench. He was no longer popular at school. There were times when he was distant and deeply depressed. Sometimes he would find a quiet place and cry for hours. However, the drugs and alcohol was still what relieved him of his pain most effectively.

CHAPTER TWENTY-THREE

Will rides his bike up to the drug spot. Several of the dealers swarm around his bike like ants on honey. Big Jay walks up to Will and asks, "What's up little man, what can I do for you? You want the usual, right?" Will acknowledged that he wanted the usual but told him he wanted more this time. Big Jay figured he could get more bang for his bucks by schooling Will on how to make crack.

"Well, look man, why don't you let me show you a way for you to take this shit a little further? If you make this shit into rocks you will be much better off, trust me. Hell, I can guarantee you will be back soon for more. The players can keep getting it their regular way, but I am telling you this is good little man," Big Jay said. "Just Park your bike and I'll take care of you," Big Jay continued.

Will parked his bike in the yard. He went inside the small house cautiously and nervously. The house was in pretty bad shape on the inside. It was very dirty and disorganized. Big Jay takes Will to the kitchen and pulls out a chair for Will to sit in. There are several other drug dealers at the table. They are laughing and joking with each other as they gamble and play cards.

There are several items on the table to convert the cocaine to crack form. There are some bags of powdered cocaine and some crack rocks. "Little man, you see how easy that shit is to make. All you need is the coke, baking soda, water and some ice cubes. Man, you got all that shit in your kitchen, minus the coke," Big Jay said. "How do you take it?" Will inquired.

Big Jay looked at Will, then looked at his other boys and said, "You just get you a tube, push one of these down in it as a filter and you smoke it. Yeah man, I can show you how to do all that. You just make sure you introduce it to some cats you know. We can give you a good deal on this shit." Big Jay proceeded to call Will over and actually show him how to make the crack cocaine. Will could see how easy it was to make the crack. He also saw how it could be profitable, as he helped package it.

The next week, at the high school, Will was in the principal's office. Will is in a lot of trouble and it does not look good for him. He looks notably upset. Mr. Roberts is standing over him looking down at him with a mean look. "I got your ass this time Will! You're out of here. I knew it would just be a matter of time before you slipped up," Mr. Roberts said. Will started crying. He is just not able to contain himself and the tears began to flow freely.

PREDATOR ON THE DIAMOND: THE BOSTON RED SOX YOUTH MOLESTATION STORY

"Come on Mr. Roberts, can't you give me another chance? My mother is going to kill me," Will pleaded. "Hell no! You bring dope in my school and think because you're on the team; you can get away with it. You have been acting up in your classes and coming to school when you feel like it. Your mother will not respond to me despite all my letters and attempts to contact her. You see, that's exactly why I don't want your kind in my school. You turn our nice schools into ghetto schools with your drugs, gangs and graffiti all over the Goddamn place. And worst yet you all are a bad influence on the good kids we have here," Mr. Roberts responded. Will continued to beg and plead with Mr. Roberts.

He apologized to Mr. Roberts several more times and told him his mother was very ill. Mr. Roberts told Will he had a good mind to have him arrested. He told Will, he did not want him in the school anymore. Will being expelled only two years before graduating, would be another painful chapter opened in his life. "Okay, Mr. Roberts I'll just leave right now," Will said as he continued to cry. "Here is just a little warning to you. When you do leave, I don't ever want to see you back in my school again. If I do, you will be taken into custody by security, and arrested for trespassing. Understood?" Mr. Roberts said.

Will told Mr. Roberts he understood, and he would not return. Mr. Roberts told Will to empty all his lockers. He then advised Will; he would attempt to contact his mother to come get him. "I can't let you leave until your mother comes for you," Mr. Roberts said. Will had turned around and prepared to leave. "Hold on a second Will. I'm going to have security take you to get your things. Then, they will escort you outside, and wait with you until your mother comes to get you." Will flops back down in his seat with an attitude and gives Mr. Roberts a mean look. "I told you my mom is sick. I can get home myself," Will said.

Mr. Roberts told Will he could not let him leave by himself. Will had to think fast. He told Mr. Roberts his older brother would come get him. Mr. Roberts told Will that would be fine. He allowed Will to use the office telephone to call his brother. "I don't think you'll be working with the Red Sox much longer either. I'm going to make sure they get notified about your conduct here at school," Mr. Roberts warned. "Why are you doing this to me? I wasn't selling the drugs to anyone," Will protested. Mr. Roberts looked at Will with disdain and said, "Look, just save it! You people are all the same. I don't need to sit here and listen to your flimsy excuses. Goddamn it, you're out of here! I'm sure you're familiar with that term since you work out at the ballpark."

CHAPTER TWENTY-FOUR

In the home-side locker room, there are several players sitting on the bench after a ball game. The clubbies pick up clothes and equipment. They also tidy up the locker room. Will is noticeably upset and nearly in tears. The tension around him can be cut with a knife. He approaches one of the baseball players, Dan, but he just ignores him and walks away. Will wants to regain the trust of the players. He had lost his connection with the players who he thought so highly of and loved working with.

Dan came back to give Will a piece of his mind. "Man, you should be ashamed of yourself. I thought you were a good clubby, hell, we all thought you were a good clubby. Shit, we treated you like you were family, and you do this," the player admonishes Will. The players all leave, as Will sits on the bench, folds his arms and starts crying. The other clubbies just sweep and clean around him, as if he is a statue. Fitzy, who was standing there observing everything, walks up and sits next to Will. "Hey buddy, pull yourself together," Fitzy said as he handed Will a handkerchief.

Will stopped crying momentarily. The other clubbies stood there looking at him. Fitzy told them to go clean another area. They all left slowly, not wanting to leave Will alone with Fitzy. Fitzy puts his finger over his own lips to give Will the hush sign. Fitzy wanted to make sure all the clubbies left before they talked. After they left, Will said, "You said you would take care of me!" Fitzy replied, "Whoa little buddy, we need to talk somewhere more private. Follow me." Will followed Fitzy into the training room of the clubhouse. Will no longer seemed to have the fear of being alone with Fitzy like he once had. When Fitzy goes in there with Will, the other clubbies all disperse, as if there was a bomb threat.

Fitzy closed the door and said, "Look, I have no control of what the folks around here do and say. Now, I have saved your ass so many times it's not funny. But you run your mouth too much buddy. I make you my number one clubby and you go telling the players what was supposed to be our secret. You almost got me in some serious trouble because that got back to management. I never hurt you buddy. I have always helped you. Hell, I've given you over a thousand dollars out of my pocket. That's way more than any other clubby. I've helped you, your mother, your brother, and your whole damn family."

PREDATOR ON THE DIAMOND: THE BOSTON RED SOX YOUTH MOLESTATION STORY

Will stood there silently for a minute. He needed the one man in the organization, who he once feared and disliked so much, to help him. "But, you said you would take care of me and help me out whenever I needed you. Right now, I need you to help me, because they might let me go. I don't want them to let me go," Will pleaded. "I don't think I can fix this! I told you about those drugs when you got caught the first time. I let you guys drink, chew tobacco and smoke cigarettes all you want, but I told you to leave that shit alone. Now, you told somebody in management the drugs were for the players. Nobody there believes that." The truth was the drugs were for the players, him, and even other clubbies.

However, he was the only clubby coming forth with these types of allegations. It seemed the other clubbies were afraid of what might happen if they told on Fitzy or the players. Many of them looked up to the players. Some were even looking up to Fitzy. "Please, could you at least talk to them? I am willing to do whatever you want. I'll even let you play the daddy game with me," Will pleaded. Fitzy just sort of chuckled, and said, "As tempting as that sounds, I still won't be able to help you. Now the players and management all want you out of here. This was your last game, so you need to pack your things and move out buddy. I have a big strong guy who is going to take your place tomorrow from the home side."

"I might just make him my number one clubby. Now as for you buddy, I wish all the best for you. Like I said, there's nothing I can do for you," Fitzy continued. Will needed Fitzy to listen to him and understand his situation. He began to cry like a baby. Look buddy, if you need anything from me, you know where to find me. Now I have a job to do so, I need to get going," Fitzy told Will. Fitzy walked out. Several clubbies walked in to see if Will was okay. They saw Will crying and asked him what was wrong. Will responded to them by letting them know he would no longer be working there.

The other clubbies attempted to console him, but there was really nothing they could say or do to change things. The next day, Will was just relaxing and sitting on the couch watching television. Shirley has returned to work on a part-time basis. She comes in from work very tired and upset. She flings a bag of groceries on the table. "Will, what are you doing?" She asked, as she stood there looking at him. Will knew where the question was going, but answered saying, "I'm watching television momma." Shirley definitely did not lose her disciplinary stance around the house. Will would have to pull his weight around the house.

"Oh no! You're not going to just sit around here and rot away. You need to get off your ass and do something. You can get a job, or you can go to the military," Shirley said. Will was so into the television program he completely ignored Shirley. Shirley then walked over to the television and turned it off. "Momma I'm too young for the military," Will reminded Shirley. Shirley just looked at Will angrily as she put her hand on her hip. She may be still sick, but her maternal instincts were still very much alive. "Boy don't get smart with me! Your next option is to go with your daddy," she said loudly.

Will told his mother he was just watching television and he was not bothering anybody. Shirley did not like the tone of Will's voice. She was not accustomed to this type of behavior from Will. "Go to your room since you want to be smart. You are not going to be coming in and out of this house at all hours of the night. I know you're out there messing with them damn drugs. All they're doing is screwing up your head," Shirley warned. Will wondered how his mother knew so much. There were times when he felt she had some sort of powers. However, he planned to talk to his brother to see if he told her.

Will kicked over the coffee table and asked, "Why doesn't everyone just leave me alone?" Shirley goes to the kitchen and picks up a broom. She takes it out to the living room where Will is now standing. "Now that's it, I've had it with you!" Shirley says as she goes after Will with the broom. Will grabs the broom from her and raises it as if he is going to strike her. Jimmy, who has heard the commotion and came downstairs, jumps in and wrestles the broom away from Will. They get into a fight. Will storms in the kitchen to get a knife. When he comes back out Jimmy and Shirley start backing up. Will had a rather large butcher's knife.

He swings the knife towards them, backing them into a corner. "I told you all to leave me alone!" Will yelled. "Will, you put that knife down or I will have your ass locked up. You have lost your mind boy." Will turns around and heads to the front door. He throws the knife so hard that it sticks perfectly in the wall like a dart. He storms out of the house, slamming the door behind himself. Shirley opens the door and yells, "Don't come back here! I mean it! You can come back and get your things, but I want you out of here. You can go to your father's house or to a shelter, I don't care!" Will grabs his bike, starts to take off and yells, "Just leave me alone!" Shirley slammed the door and stood there breathing hard for a while. She is still in shock from the encounter.

"Those drugs done made that boy crazy! I don't want his ass back in here. I'm through with him. I'm out here working like a dog to provide for you all and he's about to destroy the family. If he comes back here I want the police called, understood?" "Yes, I understand," Jimmy replied. Shirley just flopped down on the couch, still breathing hard from the encounter. "Lordy! Lordy! Lordy! I'm going to lose my baby!" She yells out as she begins to cry uncontrollably.

Jimmy sits next to Shirley and tries to comfort her. "Momma, it's going to be okay. Maybe we can get him some help," he said. Jimmy wanted to tell his mother about what he knew was going on at the ballpark. He knew it was somehow connected to Will's behavior. He was molested by Fitzy, and he knew Will and Larry were too. For some reason, Jimmy and Larry's abuse did not cause them to act out to this point, but it later would.

They both were better at concealing their feelings. However, they were in just as much pain as Will. Jimmy decided to spare his mother the pain of knowing what happened to them. Later that evening, Will was inside Fitzy's room at the Holiday Inn with a hand full of dollars. He stands there counting his money, which was given to him by Fitzy. Will had acquired lots of gifts and cash from Fitzy and the players over time.

Fitzy and the players had provided him with watches, autographed sports memorabilia, cash and even clothes. Will picked up his bike, which was leaning against the wall, unlatched all the locks and chains on the door, and started rolling his bike out into the hallway. Fitzy peaked out of the half-opened room door with a grin on his face. "Will, you're still my number one clubby! Buddy, you're always welcomed over here! If you can't find a shelter to stay at, you are certainly welcomed here. You don't have to stay with me, but I can get you a room here at the Holiday Inn."

Fitzy even offered to fly Will out to Boston to be his personal assistant at the Fenway Park clubhouse. He told Will he was irreplaceable as a clubby and would be sorely missed if he could not work at one of the ballparks. Will stopped briefly to make sure he heard Fitzy right. Will really needed to get out of Winter Haven, and he felt this might be a good opportunity. Will just waved bye to Fitzy and continued walking his bike through the lobby and out the front door. Will pulls out a small bottle of liquor and guzzles it down, as he walks his bike. He then takes out a marijuana joint, lights it, and starts smoking it as he rides away with his bike. He was now using drugs and alcohol to numb his pain more than ever. He had even tried the crack cocaine from "The Spot".

CHAPTER TWENTY-FIVE

The year is now 1991. Fitzy enters the front office. Several members of the Red Sox management staff are sitting at a table. They have some bad news for Fitzy, as one of them gestures for Fitzy to have a seat. The tension is pretty thick in the room as they look through some papers. The management staff is comprised of several Caucasian men. One of the gentlemen, Harry, told Fitzy they had to let him go. Fitzy was finally exposed when a boy showed up at the ballpark with a big sign.

The sign read, "Donald Fitzpatrick molested me." This was at a nationally televised game. "Well, we have heard from the clubbies, and they say you touch them and sexually harass them. Hell, even a few players have confirmed what they say. I mean, we can't let this go on anymore. Now this young boy has come forward with these allegations. This could do a lot of damage to the organization," Harry advised Fitzy. Fitzy was in the organization since he was a teenage boy himself. He was at the tender age of fifteen and had grown into adulthood with the Red Sox. He felt he needed to defend his honor. "Look Harry, I treat those boys well. I have been in this organization for a long time, and I have left a lasting impression on every team that's come here. Our clubbies are the best clubbies in baseball.

I took most of them from the ghetto and gave them a sense of pride," Fitzy reminded them as his eyes began to well up with tears. Fitzy truly believed he was doing more good than harm to these young boys. "Well, we appreciate your contributions to this organization and their contributions as well. Now, we can call it a resignation or a retirement, whichever you like. Therefore, we are not officially firing you. You get to leave quietly, and honorably, without stirring up too much controversy," Harry told Fitzy as he thumbed through the papers, peering over his glasses.

Fitzy wanted to know if he needed to leave right away. They let him know the sooner and quieter, the better. Fitzy stood up and the three gentlemen also stood up. They each shook Fitzy's hand. Fitzy just turned around, almost military style, shook his head and walked away. Will is twenty-one years old now. He smokes crack cocaine and drinks heavily. He has been in prison several times for various crimes.

His grandmother has passed away, as well as his father. His other two brothers had moved out and moved on. His sister, Lisa, is now sixteen. She was being raised by Shirley in the same house. She was set to graduate the next year and was doing well in school. Will did go back home every now and then because Shirley loved him so much. She would always take Will in. She felt guilty and thought that Will's problems were mainly because of the absence of his father.

Will still had not told her about what happened to him at the ballpark. Four years later, in 1995, Will met and married Renee. Renee married Will, even though she knew he had problems. She fell in love with Will's "bad boy" image. Renee had some baggage too, as she grew up watching her father abuse her mother. Her mother had a strong faith, and so did Renee. Renee felt she could change Will for the better through her faith, and with help from the good Lord.

After all, that was how she endured what she went through, and became the successful woman she was. On many occasions, Renee would show up in an alley, shelter, or crack house and pull Will out. She would take him home and dry him out. She would even bail him out of jail. She tried sending him to get help with his drug and alcohol addiction, with no success. He had never told Renee, at least to this point, about his sexual abuse at the ballpark. When Renee began to have children by Will, this behavior became more prevalent. Over the years they had two kids. They were blessed with a boy and a girl.

CHAPTER TWENTY-SIX

Once again, we go back to the Psychiatrist's office in Florida, in the year 2001. Will had set aside an empty box of what used to be tissues. He uses up the only tissue he has left to dry his face. "Well Will, that is quite a story. I'm sure that's not the end of it, so if you feel like going on, you still have lots of time," Doctor Ross said as he looked at his watch, then the clock. The doctor reached down in his bottom draw and pulled out a fresh box of tissues.

"Well, basically, my wife Renee, pretty much saved my life. We are still together to this day. She refused to give up on me. I remember times when she dragged my butt to church, when I had a hangover, or had just come off a crack binge. She would have half the church praying over me, as if I was possessed by the devil." "Wow, that's pretty interesting. You said you had two kids with her too right?" Will said, "That's correct, a boy and a girl. Their names are Wanda and Phillip. Wanda is six and Phillip is four." Doctor Ross asked Will how they were doing. Will told him they're actually doing really well considering all they have been through. "As I said, they have a real strong woman for a mother. I'm actually very close to them now, and I refuse to let what happened to me happen to either one of them. I am very protective of them," Will said.

PREDATOR ON THE DIAMOND: THE BOSTON RED SOX YOUTH MOLESTATION STORY

Doctor Ross knew these questions may be intrusive, but he wanted Will to really be able to open up to him. "So how do you feel this affected your life overall? I mean the molestation by Fitzy, and the introduction of the drugs to you by the players," Doctor Ross clarified. Will's eyes begin to tear up again. It is clear that he has not fought many of the demons stemming from his childhood. "I tried every drug in the book including prescription. I was headed for self-destruction. As I said, I even spent some time in and out of "the joint," I finally realized I needed help, and that I didn't want that lifestyle anymore. I knew the drugs weren't helping me escape my past. So, I just stopped taking them. I was even in and out of mental institutions several times.

One thing I never did was actually tell my story and get help for what happened to me. I just feel ready now. I have been completely clean for over two years now. It still gets shaky every now and then, so I just take one day at a time," Will said. Doctor Ross scribbled some notes on the pad he had in front of him. "It sounds like you have come a long way. I can introduce you to some actual victims groups. Most of them use group therapy sessions. You will get to share your experiences with other victims of rape, abuse and molestation," Doctor Ross said. Will had to think for a while and was therefore quiet. He did not know if he was ready to expose his most intimate and delicate secrets in a group setting. "I would appreciate that," Will finally agreed.

Doctor Ross asked Will if he knew how some of the other ex-clubbies and victims were doing right now. "Well, some of them are in prison, some are drug addicts, and some are pedophiles or convicted rapists themselves. They're basically acting out what they experienced. Some are now deceased. When I go back to my neighborhood, I see some of them living the street life. I didn't even recognize some of them," Will responded. Doctor Ross said, "I think you have quite a story that needs to be told. I mean to the country or maybe even the world." "Maybe I should look into that," Will said. Doctor Ross shook his head, still in disbelief and said, "Telling your story could be quite therapeutic, not to mention lucrative. Perhaps you should even seek legal counsel to see what options you have for seeking restitution."

He went on to tell Will he was not sure about the laws as far as the statute of limitation. "I never thought about that before. I never even told anyone about my experiences, not even my mother or wife. I just kept it inside of me, thinking I could deal with it on my own. I worried about what people might think. I had a lot of problems and confusion dealing with my sexuality," Will said. Doctor Ross told Will that what he was experiencing was not unusual, and that it was not unusual to blame himself for what happened. He also explained the term Stockholm syndrome to Will, and how it may affect a victim in relation to the abuser.

He told Will that was most likely why he went to Boston to stay with Fitzy on several occasions. "So where is Fitzy now?" Doctor Ross asked. "I don't know if he is even alive. He would be pretty old if he is, maybe in his seventies. He may be still living somewhere in Boston," Will responded. Doctor Ross once again pauses, looks at the clock on the wall, then his watch. He told Will to set up another appointment with him through his secretary.

CHAPTER TWENTY-SEVEN

Will was back home having a conversation with Renee. Will finally told his wife what happened to him when he was younger. She felt it was many years too late, and she was upset, because she had to hear about it on the news. She was even more upset because he held a secret from her for so long. "So, Will, when did you plan on telling me about this?" Renee asked. Will, with a confused look, said "I don't know honey. I may have never told you."

Renee felt she could have gotten Will some help sooner. Will was apologetic but let her know that was just not a subject a man wants to talk about with his wife. He feared what she would think about him. "So, everything we went through over the years wasn't because of your father. It was because of this dirty old white man, right?" Renee asked. Will answered Renee saying, "I didn't want you to find out about it like this, through the media. Like I said, I am sorry." Renee walked away crying, as Will tried to stop her and comfort her.

PREDATOR ON THE DIAMOND: THE BOSTON RED SOX YOUTH MOLESTATION STORY

Weeks later, Will has come to talk to Doctor Ross once again. Doctor Ross asked Will how things were going now that his story had been told. Will shook his head and said, "It's been like hell! Shit, my wife hardly speaks to me anymore. She doesn't have the desire to make love to me much either. She thinks I'm gay, bi or on the down low. She even had us both take HIV tests." Doctor Ross thought she was over-reacting a bit, but he could understand her being upset. He quickly changed the subject by asking Will what the outcome was for the case. He had heard bits and pieces of the case in the news just like everyone else.

Will said he acquired a lawyer, and that at this point they were prepared to file a lawsuit. "How does that make you feel?" Doctor Ross asked. Will was clearly still upset about what Fitzy had done to him years earlier. His resentment was notable. After all, he felt this man had caused him a lifetime of problems. "I think he is going to lie his way out of it. I thought about getting a gun, going to Massachusetts, and blasting his old ass! The "Curse of the Bambino" ain't even got shit on me," Will proclaimed. Doctor Ross looked at Will with a sort of surprised expression and said, "I see. So, you basically feel like taking Fitzy out, right?"

Will felt he needed to retract that statement. He could see how Doctor Ross might think he was a few cards short of a full deck for telling him that. "Don't worry, Doctor Ross, I'm not going to really shoot him. That would be too quick," Will said. Doctor Ross asked, "What happened to the guy who held up the sign at the ballpark? It seems he really was the one who put an end to all of this. You said Mister Fitzpatrick resigned after that." "Rumor has it they gave that guy one hundred thousand dollars. I haven't heard anything about where he is now or what happened to him," Will said.

"So, other than the potential lawsuit, what do you plan on doing with your life?" Doctor Ross asked. "We do have a few more minutes," He continued. Will had to think for a second, but then said, "I don't know. I hope to be able to stay clean and continue to let God take care of me. I want to talk to other youth and educate them about molesters and pedophiles. I want to also help adults who are dealing with the pain and are trying to cope with sexual abuse in their past. I don't want anyone to suffer like I have. Maybe I can get on the Oprah Show or the Doctor Phil Show." Doctor Ross told him that was a good idea.

He also told Will, it may help him cope with his own molestation, and perhaps give him some closure. Will let the doctor know that he had done quite a bit of studying up on predators. How they think, who they prey on, some of the ways they operate, and so on and so forth. "I don't allow my kids to associate with too many adults. I don't let them spend the night at anyone's house, not even relatives. I read that a large portion of molestations, sexual abuse and rapes take place by someone known by the victim, or an actual family member," Will said.

Doctor Ross shook his head yes, and said, "That's very true. It happens all the time, but I guess one can go overboard, and believe it or not, become overprotective or paranoid." Doctor Ross looks at his watch, and then the clock on the wall, and said, "I guess that will conclude this session. I will schedule you as needed," Doctor Ross said. He handed Will a list of organizations as he had promised. Will thanked Doctor Ross for everything and shook his hand. "Oh, by the way, I forgot to tell you, I joined the Fresh Start program for victims of sexual abuse," Will said proudly. "That's great! Speaking of programs, have you ever got help for your drug and alcohol problem?" Doctor Ross inquired. He knew Will could not keep trying to deal with his pain by relapsing into drug use.

Will reluctantly answered with a low tone saying, "No Doctor Ross, I think I can beat that myself. I mean, it has been a struggle for me over the years, but I am sure I can beat it. Believe me if I don't beat it my wife will beat me." Doctor Ross advised Will that in his professional opinion, he believes he should get some help for that too. "Trust me Doc, I will be fine. I'm moving from Florida with my family, whenever this lawsuit is filed and goes through. Who knows, the change of scenery may be just what I need," Will said as he started to ease towards the door. Doctor Ross knew Will had his card and contact info, but he still handed Will another business card. "Okay, but if you ever do decide to get substance abuse help, just let me know. I know a lot of places you can go," he reminded Will. Will waved his hand with acknowl- edgement of the doctor, as he quickly exited. Unfortunately, Will did not believe he needed help for his past drug and alcohol problems.

CHAPTER TWENTY-EIGHT

On September 12, 2001, a day after the terror attacks on the twin towers, a class action lawsuit was filed against the Boston Red Sox. At that time there were seven victims, who were now grown, who came forward. Will was not named in the lawsuit. They became known as "The Winter Haven Seven." They each had their own counsel, and their lawyers were skeptical, because of the years that had passed since the molestations occurred. They were seeking 3.15 million dollars in damages for this case.

Eight months later, on May 16, 2002, Donald Fitzpatrick pleads guilty to four counts of attempted sexual battery, after Polk County launched a criminal investigation. He was given a ten-year suspended sentence and fifteen years' probation. Now, 72 years old, he returned to Massachusetts a free man. They all agreed to this except for Will, and one or two other victims. Will and his lawyer would fight for a bigger settlement.

On May 28, 2003, a little over a year later, the victims were paid the settlement. The settlement was made by the now new Boston Red Sox ownership. Will and his lawyer refused the settlement, because one of the conditions of the settlement was, they were not allowed to tell their stories. They also felt the settlement offer was too low.

In 2005, two years later, Donald Fitzpatrick passed away. Will's case still had not settled. However, Will was able to find someone to help him get his story told. He was able to find a ghostwriter to help him get a book out about his experiences as a clubbie in the Red Sox organization. The book was entitled, "Predator on the Diamond: The Boston Red Sox Youth Molestation Story."

Later that year, Will was on a stage in a large conference room. He is dressed in a dark colored business suit. There is a large crowd of people in the room, and some people are standing, as there is standing room only. There is a large banner hanging above the stage that reads, "Introducing the novel Predator on the Diamond: The Boston Red Sox Youth Molestation Story by William Jones." Many of the people from the audience have brought their children with them. Will's family is seated in the front row (His wife, mother, kids, brothers, their kids and his sister).

PREDATOR ON THE DIAMOND: THE BOSTON RED SOX YOUTH MOLESTATION STORY

Will does have his counsel with him, and he is a middle-aged African American man. He is sitting in a chair on the stage next to Will. There is a large table situated on the side of the room with a couple of chairs. There are hundreds of books on the table. An African American man, steps to the podium and clears his throat. The people in the audience, who are seated, join the ones who are standing, and they all applaud. "Thank you. I know you all are not applauding for me, but I still want to thank you. Without further ado, I present to you winner of an African American Achievement Award. Author of the bestselling novel, Predator on the Diamond: The Boston Red Sox Youth Molestation Story... William Jones."

As Will stands and heads towards the podium, he once again gets a standing ovation. He clears his throat and suddenly there is silence again. "Thank you. First of all, I want to thank God for blessing me and helping me get through this ordeal. I owe a lot to my family and my beautiful wife. They all stood by me." The audience applauds once again. He continued, "Of course I want to thank you all for supporting me and making my story a best seller." He told them he felt like a huge weight has been lifted off him. He plans to continue this journey and mission so to speak. He plans to save one life at a time by bringing awareness to this problem.

"I only hope and pray that no other child has to go through what I did, and what the other clubbies went through." There is a few seconds of silence, and then the sound of applause breaks the silence. The audience stands up and gives Will a standing ovation. Will flips through the pages of his notes and continues. "Parents please take a more active role in raising your children. If you don't, you leave the door open for anyone who wants to prey on them. It can change their lives forever. Now, I don't blame my mother for this at all. She had to raise us by herself. She had to practically stay at work just to make ends meet. So, I know there are situations where it can be difficult for parents."

"Be sure to warn your children about predators and pedophiles. Tell them what actions they should take if someone touches them or does something inappropriate to them. Yeah, I know you hear about child molestations in the news quite a bit now. But please, I say again please, do not think it won't happen to your child. And yes, I know we want to get our children involved in sports and other activities. I say we continue doing that with a watchful eye on our children. Now, I have lots of copies of my book, and I will be signing them for you in just a moment. I will also be answering any questions you may have. Thank you all once again."

There is a standing ovation once again and Will makes his way to the table with the books. He then takes a seat with his counsel. News cameras follow him all the way. Flashing lights can be seen coming from dozens of cameras. The media is even present with their cameras and press passes visible around their necks. People begin to form a line, in an orderly fashion, to get their copy of Will's book.

CHAPTER TWENTY-NINE

Months later, Will is still living near the Winter Haven, Florida area, although he and his wife and kids have moved to a nicer area. The book sales have been very good. There is even talk of a film by Tyler Film Productions. On a warm summer's evening, a black 2005 Cadillac Escalade pulls up to a known drug spot. It just sits there parked for a while. The drug dealers, four African American teens on the corner, keep a watchful eye on the vehicle as they continue selling their drugs.

One of the dealers approaches the car. He knocks on the driver's side window, which has a very dark tint. "Hey man, you buying or what?" The dealer asked. The window rolls down slowly, and Will's face can be seen. "No young man, I am not buying." The dealer backs up slowly and looks around for an escape route. "Are you a cop or something?" He inquired. Will smirked and said, "No, I am not a cop. I just came by here to give you guys something."

PREDATOR ON THE DIAMOND: THE BOSTON RED SOX YOUTH MOLESTATION STORY

Will gets out and opens the back of his SUV. The drug dealer follows Will to the back of the SUV. There are dozens of copies of his book. "What do you got there man?" The drug dealer asked Will. Will picks up a book and shows it to the drug dealer. Reading the title aloud, the drug dealer said, "Predator on the Diamond. . . Oh, you're that dude named William Jones!" Will acknowledged that he was correct, and the dealer asked Will what he was doing out there. Will handed him the book and said, "Here, this is for you. It's autographed. In fact, they're all autographed."

The dealer takes the book and looks it over. "Cool, you sure you don't want nothing for this man?" The dealer asked. "Yeah, I'm positive. I don't need that stuff anymore. In fact, take as many as you want. Pass them out to your boys," Will said. The dealer took a few more books. He read the back cover synopsis for the book and asked, "Are you trying to put me out of business or something man? I don't want no inspirational shit working on them. That was some heavy shit that happened to you man." "I'm just sharing my life with folks. What you guys do with your life and the choices you make are strictly up to you," Will advised the dealer. Will gets in his car, rolls up his super dark tinted windows, and cruises away.

The dealer just stands there looking in disbelief. The other dealers go up to him, taking the books from him. They all start flipping through the pages of the book. The first dealer starts collecting the books back. "You all don't need to read that shit. I'm going to throw these books away. Hell, maybe I can sell them. You fools can't read anyway!" He said. He puts the books into his backpack. They all walk away and continue selling their drugs.

Months later, Will is being interviewed at a sports news studio. Once again, he wears a suit and tie. He is there with his lawyer. There is an African American female reporter, Melody Smith, sitting next to Will and his lawyer. "What do you expect to see happen with this lawsuit you have filed against the Boston Red Sox?" She asked. "I expect to win. I will not rest until they take responsibility for allowing that man to steal my childhood and my innocence," Will responded. The reporter looked down at her paper and asked, "How do you feel about these other stories of sexual abuse, like the recent Jackson case, where he was of course acquitted, and other cases like the church scandal?" Will said, "The message that needs to be clear is that it doesn't matter what status you achieve, whether you are a rapper, doctor, policeman, superstar, priest, sports icon or anybody else, you will pay if you molest children. And it won't necessarily be financially."

PREDATOR ON THE DIAMOND: THE BOSTON RED SOX YOUTH MOLESTATION STORY

"No amount of money can change the lifetime of mental trauma I will suffer. This isn't just about the money. If it was, I could have joined the other victims in the class action lawsuit three years ago. No, I want my story to be heard. Not just with my book, but in the judicial system. These sports organizations should be held accountable when they don't protect these kids, and instead choose to protect the predator," Will continued. "You have sort of become the spokesperson for molestation, rape and sexual abuse victims, right?" She asked.

Will told her he definitely didn't mind wearing that hat. "We also want to get the system to work better for the victim. The victim should not become victimized by the justice system," Will said. The reporter started to wrap things up as she said, "We certainly wish you well in your endeavors, Mr. Jones, and congratulations on your book becoming a bestseller. She holds a copy of Will's book up to the camera and says, "Predator on the Diamond: The Boston Red Sox Youth Molestation Story is available at bookstores now. Once again, thanks for your time." "No problem. Thank you," Will said.

The reporter turns, looks into the camera and says, "It looks like Mr. Jones may have an uphill battle. There will be many questions that need to be answered. We'll definitely keep you updated on this powerful story as it unfolds. Melody Smith, live from Studio One Sports. Now back to Tom at the sports news desk.

EPILOGUE

Will never received compensation from the Boston Red Sox. Unfortunately, because he never received help for his cocaine problem, he again relapsed. He spent more time in prison. His wife could no longer go through it, and she left with the kids. She later divorced him and took custody of the children. His mother stayed in Winter Haven. She was no longer able to work because her health deteriorated. Lisa, now 30, ironically became a nurse and takes care of her. Larry took his own life and Jimmy ended up in a mental institution.

The stories of the other victims were very similar. Most of them were not able to overcome the problems linked to the sexual abuse. However, a few did. More victims have come forward since the initial lawsuit was filed. There have been more laws implemented to deal with pedophiles since this case. However, these stories of sexual abuse in churches, schools, and sports institutions are still prevalent. Hopefully, telling these stories and exposing these pedophiles, as well as the organizations that harbor them, will help. Parents need to take a more active role in raising their children and educating them about pedophiles. Hopefully this story will help bring awareness to this issue.

Gary G. Tavares

Red Sox Statement on Donald Fitzpatrick

Mr. Fitzpatrick served as the team's clubhouse manager from the 1960s until 1991, and the actions you have inquired about occurred between 1971 and 1991. When the team, then under a previous ownership group, became aware of the allegations against Mr. Fitzpatrick in 1991, he was promptly relieved of his duties. Civil litigation was filed in 2001, by victims of Mr. Fitzpatrick, for actions that had occurred more than 20 years earlier. The team, which was acquired by the current ownership group after the lawsuit was filed, reached a settlement in 2002. Mr. Fitzpatrick has since passed away. The Red Sox have always viewed the actions of Mr. Fitzpatrick to be abhorrent.

THE END

CHILD MOLESTATION STATISTICS

"The serial killer has the same personality characteristics as the sex offender against children"-Dr. Mace Knapp, Nevada State Prison Psychologist.

• "There are 400,000 registered sex offenders in the United States, and an estimated 80 to 100,000 of them are missing. They're supposed to be registered, but we don't know where they are, and we don't know where they're living. - Ernie Allen, President of the National Center for Missing and Exploited Children to co-anchor Hannah Storm on *The Early Show*

• The most serious and chronic offenders often show signs of antisocial behavior as early as the preschool years. - (American Psychiatric Association, 1994) (was in Juvenile Justice Bulletin: Nov 1998 OJJDP: U.S. Department of Justice)

• Dr. Gene Abel estimates that between 1% and 5% of our population molest children -CNN Specials Transcript #454-Thieves of Childhood.

• Nearly all the offenders in sexual assaults reported to law enforcement were male (96%). - Sexual Assault of Young Children as Reported to Law Enforcement, 7/00, NCJ 182990, U.S. Department of Justice

• Overall, 23% of sexual assault offenders were under the age of 18 and 77% were adults - Sexual Assault of Young Children as Reported to Law Enforcement, 7/00, NCJ 182990, U.S. Department of Justice

• 40% of the offenders of victims under age 6 were themselves juveniles. A similar proportion (39%) of offenders of victims ages 6 through 11 were also juveniles. For older juvenile victims, the proportion of juvenile offenders dropped to 27%. - Sexual Assault of Young Children as Reported to Law Enforcement, 7/00, NCJ 182990, U.S. Department of Justice

•Adults were the offender in 60% of the sexual assaults of youth under age 12. Rarely were the offenders of young victims strangers. Strangers were the offender in just 3% of sexual assaults against victims under age 6 and 5% of the sexual assault of victimizations of youth ages 6 through 11. -Sexual Assault of Young Children as Reported to Law Enforcement,7/00, NCJ 182990, U.S. Department of Justice

• 1 in 5 violent offenders serving time in a state prison reported having victimized a child.-BJS Survey of State Prison Inmates, 1991.

• 2/3 of all prisoners convicted of rape or sexual assault had committed their crime against a child.-BJS Survey of State Prison Inmates, 1991.

• Acquaintance perpetrators are the most common abusers, constituting approximately 70-90% of all reported perpetrators.-Finkelhor, D. 1994.

• 89% of child sexual assault cases involve persons known to the child, such as a caretaker or family acquaintance.- Diana Russell Survey, 1978

• 29% of child sexual abuse offenders are relatives, 60% are acquaintances, and only 11% are strangers.-Diana Russell, *The Secret Trauma*, NY: Basic Books, 1986.

• For the vast majority of child victimizers in State prison, the victim was someone they knew before the crime. 1/3 had committed their crime against their own child, about 1/2 had a relationship with the victim as a friend, acquaintance, or relative other than offspring, about 1 in 7 reported the victim to have been a stranger to them. -BJS Survey of State Prison Inmates, 1991.

• 3/4 of the violent victimizations of children took place in either the victim's home or the offenders home. -BJS Survey of State Prison Inmates, 1991.

• Males are reported to be the abusers in 80-95% of cases -Thoringer, D., et al., 1988.

• About 60% of the male survivors sampled report at least one of their perpetrators to be female. -Mendel, 1993.

• All but 3% of offenders who committed violent crimes against children were male. -BJS Survey of State Prison Inmates, 1991.

•The typical offender is male, begins molesting by age 15, engages in a variety of deviant behavior, and molests an average of 117 youngsters, most of whom do not report the offense. -Dr. Gene Abel in a National Institute of Mental Health Study.

• Offenders who had victimized a child were on average 5 years older than the violent offenders who had committed their crimes against adults. Nearly 25% of child victimizers were age 40 or older, but about 10% of the inmates with adult victims fell in that range. -BJS Survey of State Prison Inmates, 1991.

• 71% of male offenders are under the age of 35.-Dr. Ann Burges, Dr. Nicholas Groth, et al. in a study of imprisoned offenders.

• 3/4 of sexual predators are younger than 35. About 80% are of normal intelligence or above. -Profiles from the FBI Academy and the National Center for Missing & Exploited Children.

• Though officially, not considered abuse, the highest incidence of incest occurs among siblings. -Waterman & Lusk, 1986.

• Many clinical settings currently are witnessing a dramatic increase in the number of adolescent offenders who have committed sexually aggressive acts against other children. -Conte, Jon R., 1986.

PREDATOR ON THE DIAMOND: THE BOSTON RED SOX YOUTH MOLESTATION STORY

• While nearly 70% of those serving time for violent crimes against children were white, whites accounted for 40% of those imprisoned for violent crimes against adults. -BJS Survey of State Prison Inmates, 1991.

• Inmates who victimized children were less likely than other inmates to have a prior criminal record-nearly 1/3 of child victimizers had never been arrested prior to the current offense, compared to less than 20% of those who victimized adults. --BJS Survey of State Prison Inmates, 1991.

• Violent child victimizers were substantially more likely than those with adult victims to have been physically or sexually abused when they were children..-BJS Survey of State Prison Inmates, 1991.

• 50% of reported child molestations involve the use of physical force and child molesters produce as much visible physical injury as rapists-39% of victims. -Dr. Gene Abel in a National Institute of Mental Health Study.

• About 14% of child victimizers carried a weapon during the violent crime, compared to nearly 1/2 of those who victimized adults. -BJS Survey of State Prison Inmates, 1991.

• About 10% of violent offenders with child victims re-ceived life or death sentences and the average prison term was 11 years, somewhat shorter average sentences than received by those with adult victims.
-BJS Survey of State Prison Inmates, 1991.

• More than 1/2 of all convicted sex offenders are sent back to prison within a year. Within 2 years, 77.9% are back. - California Department of Corrections.

• Recidivism rates range from 18-45%. The more violent the crime the more likelihood of repeating. -Studies by the state of Washington.

• 3 in 10 child victimizers reported that they had committed their crimes against multiple victims: they were more likely than those who victimized adults to have had multiple victims.-BJS Survey of State Prison Inmates, 1991.

• Like rape, child molestation is one of the most underreported crimes: only 1-10% are ever disclosed.-FBI Law Enforcement Bulletin.

• The behavior is highly repetitive, to the point of compulsion, rather than resulting from a lack of judgment.-Dr. Ann Burges, Dr. Nicholas Groth et al. in a study of imprisoned offenders.

Made in United States
Orlando, FL
15 July 2023

35126926R00088